ADVANCING
SYSTEMOLOGY

KEYS TO THE KINGDOM SERIES
POCKET EDITION

THIS BOOK SHOULD NOT BE LEFT
ACCESSIBLE, IN CLEAR VIEW, OR
SHARED CASUALLY WITH OTHERS

Published from
Mardukite Borsippa HQ, San Luis Valley, Colorado
Mardukite Academy & Systemology Society
for spiritual or philosophical purposes only

ADVANCING SYSTEMOLOGY

Systemology
Advanced Training Course
Manual #8

As presented by Joshua Free
to the Systemology Society

THE JOSHUA FREE IMPRINT
JFI PUBLICATIONS

© 2024, JOSHUA FREE

ISBN : 978-1-961509-55-9

This manual is restricted to students on
The Systemology Advanced Training Course
that have already completed the
"Pathway to Ascension" Professional Course

References to prerequisite material:
Processing-Levels 0 to 6 (PC-1 to 16)
"The Secret of Universes" (AT #1)
"Games, Goals & Purposes" (AT #2)
"The Jewel of Knowledge" (AT #3)
"Implanted Universes" (AT #4)
"Entities & Fragments" (AT #5)
"Spiritual Perception" (AT #6)
"Mastering Ascension" (AT #7)

Full use of this manual may also require:
"Systemology Biofeedback"
"Systemology Procedures" and
"Systemology Piloting"

First Edition Pocket Paperback — *April 2024*

mardukite.com

The Keys to the Kingdom are Yours for the Taking!

The official Mardukite Systemology "Advanced Training Course" is now available in print for the first time.

Those Seekers that have completed the "Pathway to Ascension" Systemology Professional Course can now access the upper-level teachings of our tradition.

This book is not for everyone... This is the fourth manual for Level-8.

Never before has Joshua Free presented this material outside the confines of the Mardukite NexGen Systemology Society.

Learn how to expertly apply our spiritual technology toward reaching higher levels of Awareness and Beingness than ever before thought possible for humanity on planet Earth.

Each of the "Keys to the Kingdom" Advanced Training Course Manuals will further a Seekers reach on the Pathway leading out of this Universe.

<u>The Pathway to Ascension Professional Course</u>
#1 – *Increasing Awareness (Level-0)*
#2 – *Thought & Emotion (Level-0)*
#3 – *Clear Communication (Level-0)*
#4 – *Handling Humanity (Level-1)*
#5 – *Free Your Spirit (Level-2)*
#6 – *Escaping Spirit-Traps (Level-2)*
#7 – *Eliminating Barriers (Level-3)*
#8 – *Conquest of Illusion (Level-3)*
#9 – *Confronting the Past (Level-4)*
#10 – *Lifting the Veils (Level-4)*
#11 – *Spiritual Implants (Level-5)*
#12 – *Games and Universes (Level-5)*
#13 – *Spiritual Energy (Level-6)*
#14 – *Spiritual Machinery (Level-6)*
#15 – *The Arcs of Infinity (Level-6)*
#16 – *Alpha Thought (Level-6)*

<u>Keys to the Kingdom Advanced Training</u>
#1 – *The Secret of Universes (Level-7)*
#2 – *Games, Goals & Purposes (Level-7)*
#3 – *The Jewel of Knowledge (Level-7)*
#4 – *Implanted Universes (Level-7)*
#5 – *Entities & Fragments (Level-8)*
#6 – *Spiritual Perception (Level-8)*
#7 – *Mastering Ascension (Level-8)*
#8 – *Advancing Systemology (Level-8)*

Systemology Biofeedback
Systemology Procedures
Systemology Piloting

TABLET OF CONTENTS

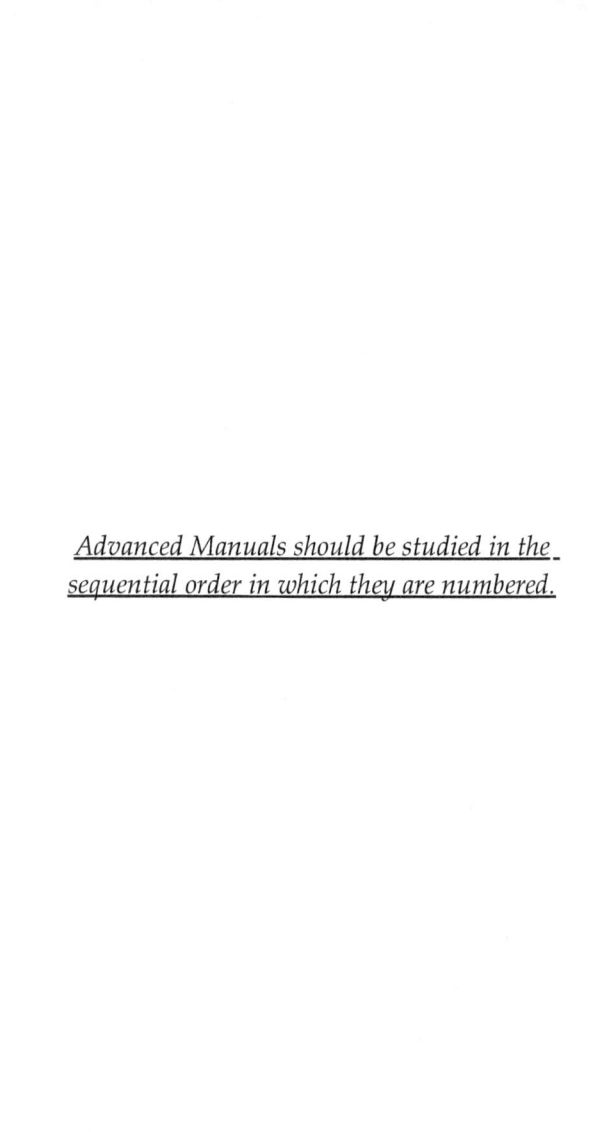

Advanced Manuals should be studied in the sequential order in which they are numbered.

INTRODUCTION TO
THE MANUAL

This manual is restricted to students on
The Systemology Advanced Training Course
that have already completed the
"Pathway to Ascension" Professional Course

References to prerequisite material:
Processing-Levels 0 to 6 (PC-1 to 16)
"The Secret of Universes" (AT #1)
"Games, Goals & Purposes" (AT #2)
"The Jewel of Knowledge" (AT #3)
"Implanted Universes" (AT #4)
"Entities & Fragments" (AT #5)
"Spiritual Perception" (AT #6)
"Mastering Ascension" (AT #7)

Full use of this manual may also require:
"Systemology Biofeedback"
"Systemology Procedures" and
"Systemology Piloting"

THE SYSTEMOLOGY
ADVANCED TRAINING COURSE
MANUAL SERIES

Mardukite Systemology is a new evolution in Human understanding about the "systems" governing *Life*, *Reality*, the *Universe* and all *Existences.* It is also a *Spiritual Path* used to transcend the Human experience and reach *"Ascension."*

This is an *Advanced Training* (*AT*) course manual detailing *upper-levels* of our spiritual philosophy. It is intended to assist *advancing* a *Seeker*'s personal progress toward the *upper-most levels* of the *Pathway.*

This manual follows after our *Professional Course* series of lessons—available as individual booklets, or collected in two volumes titled *"The Pathway to Ascension"* The *Professional Course* follows after material given in the *Basic Course* booklets, or *"Fundamentals of Systemology"* volume.

The systematic methodology that we use to assist an individual to increase their *"Actualized Awareness"* (and reach gradually higher toward their *"Spiritual Ascension"*) is referred to as *"The Pathway"* — and that individual is called a *"Seeker."*

To receive the greatest benefit from this manual: it is expected that a *Seeker* will already be familiar with the fundamental concepts and terminology (previously relayed in the *Basic Course* and *Professional Course* lessons) of our *applied philosophy.*

As a *Seeker* increases their *Awareness* in this lifetime, their spiritual *"Knowingness"* also increases—which is to say their *certainty* on *Life,* on this and other *Universes,* and on *realizing Self* as an unlimited "spiritual being" *having* an enforced restrictive "human experience." A *Seeker* also *knowingly* increases their command and control of the "human experience." And this is a part of what is meant by *"Actualized Awareness."*

CHARTING FLIGHTS ON THE PATHWAY

Although there is a systematic structure to *fragmentation,* the personal journey experienced along the *Pathway* will be different for each *Seeker.* For example, certain areas will seem more *"turbulent"* or difficult for one *Seeker* than another. We tend to say that these areas have more *"charge"* on them—or that they are more *"heavily charged."* It is best to handle such areas when you are already feeling *"good"* and not in a situation (or condition) where that specific area is consistently being *"triggered"* or *"restimulated."*

As an applied philosophy, *Systemology* "theory" can be easily utilized in the "laboratory" of the "world-at-large" in everyday life. This is implied within the basic instruction of each lesson. Unlike other "sciences" that conduct experiments by making a change to some "objective variable" *out there* and waiting to see an effect, our focus is the individual (or *Observer*) themselves, and how *they* affect the "*Reality*" perceived.

Our philosophy is applied by using specific exercises and systematic techniques. These "*processes*" provide the most stable personal gain (and *realizations*) for each area; but only when actually applied with a *Seeker's* full "*presence*" and *Awareness*. Hundreds of such *processes* may be found in the "*Pathway to Ascension*" (*Professional Course*) material.

Applying a technique is called "*running a process.*" *Processes* are designed with very simple instructions or "*command-lines.*" To *run* a *processing command-line*, a *Seeker* may be assisted by the communication of that *line* from a "*Co-Pilot*" (as in "*Traditional Piloting*"). But even then, a *Seeker* must still personally "input" the *command* as *Self.* For this reason—and quite thankfully—*Solo-Processing* is possible.

TAKING FLIGHT ON THE PATHWAY

Processing Techniques are intended to treat the *Spiritual Being* or *Alpha-Spirit*; the individual themselves. The *"command-lines"* are *directed to* the individual themselves—not some *mental machinery* of theirs, and not even a *Biofeedback* metering device.

Systematic Processing is applied by the *Alpha-Spirit*—who then *Self-directs* command of their "Mind-System" or "body" (*genetic-vehicle*), both of which are "constructs" that the *Alpha-Spirit* (*Self*, or the "I-AM" *Awareness unit*) operates, but neither of which is actually *Self*. *Fragmentation* causes *Humans* to falsely identify *Self as* the *"Mind"* or even a *"Body."*

Some *processes* can be treated quite lightly at first; others may require a bit of working at in order to get *"running"* well. It is important to set aside a period of time when you can be dedicated to your studies and *processing*. This period of time is referred to as a *"processing session."* When a *process* does start *running* well, it is important to be able to complete it to a satisfactory *"end-point."*

Processing allows us to be able to *actually* "look" at *things* and even determine the *considerations* we have made—or attitudes we have decided—about *Reality* as a result of those experiences.

It doesn't do us much good to simply "glance"—or to *restimulate* something uncomfortable and then quickly *withdraw* from it once again, leaving more of our *attention* yet again behind and held fixedly on it.

Generally speaking, a *Seeker* continues to *run* a *process* so long as something is "happening"—which is to say, the *process* is still producing a change. Usually this is evident by the type of "answers" that a *command-line* prompts a *Seeker* to originate from the database of their own *Mind-System*.

Processing Command-Lines ("PCL") are not "magic words"; they do not "do" anything on their own. They systematically assist a *Seeker* to direct their own attention toward increasing *Awareness*.

A *Seeker* may also cease to generate new "data" from a *process* without reaching an *"ultimate" realization* as an *"end-point."* It is possible that additional "layers" (or even other "areas") require handling before anything "deeper" is accessible. If this is the case, end the *process*. But, if a *Seeker* is *withdrawing* from something uncomfortable that was incited or stirred up, then a *process* is *run* until they feel "good" about it.

One of the benefits to *Flying-Solo* on the *Pathway* is that the *processing* is entirely *Self-determined*. This naturally provides a

17

certain built-in "safety" for a practitioner. Anything you *restimulate* by *Self-determinism* is *your thing*. It is not triggered or incited by some external "*other-determined*" influences (or other "source-points") that make you an *effect*. It can be more easily handled in *processing*—or you can simply let things "cool down" and come back to it again in another *session*.

While it may seem "mysterious" to beginners, a *Seeker* gets a sense for knowing how long to *run* a *process* only with practice. Once you have spent some time actually applying material from "*The Pathway to Ascension*" *Professional Course*, there are many aspects of it that become "second nature" because they are, in fact, a part of our true original native nature. All we have done in *Systemology* is "*reverse engineer*" the routes of *creation* and *consideration* that are already *our own*.

SYSTEMOLOGY LEVEL-8

We are publishing *"upper-level"* *Systemology* in 2024 for the very first time. Its effective application is dependent on a *Seeker* having already reached a stable point of *"Beta-Defragmentation."* This requires proper use of materials for *processing-levels 0 to 6*—as given in the *"Pathway to Ascension"* *Professional Course* (available in two volumes, or sixteen individual booklets).

Additionally, this current *Systemology Level-8* work is a direct continuation of *Level-7*, which *must* be completed before continuing. The *Systemology Level-7* manuals—*"The Secret of Universes," "Games, Goals & Purposes," "The Jewel of Knowledge"* and (to a lesser extent) *"Implanted Universes"*—should be treated as a single "unit" of work *prior* to approaching *Level-8*. These manuals are available individually, or as collected in *Volume One* of the *"Keys to the Kingdom" Advanced Training (A.T.) Course*.

After uncovering *"The Jewel"* and discovering the "secret" of *Universes*, a *"Seeker"* has *found* the "hidden gem" of the *Pathway* at *Level-7*, and is no longer a *"Seeker."* Of course, things are not always what we expect—and *"all that glitters is not gold."* Yet, still, it is *"The Jewel of Knowledge"* (*Parts #1-5*) and the *Entry-Point Heaven Incident*, *&tc.*, that represents the "ceiling" of *this Universe* and even what is behind it, beneath it, or embedded into its structure. It was what a *"Seeker"* had been *drawn* to in their *search*, but was never meant to find by any other method or avenue, except *systematically*.

Systemology Level-8 is the first official *"Wizard Level"* of the *Systemology Society*. As stated in *A.T. Manual #4*: while "formal" *Advanced Training* may end with manuals representing *Systemology Level-8* (and completing the *"Keys to the Kingdom"* series), this will also open up, what is referred to by the *Mardukite Academy* as, the *"Infinity Grade."* [For instructional purposes, we tend to still refer to a practitioner as a *"Seeker"* in the *upper-level* manuals.]

There is no finite end-point to the *"Infinity Grade"* because its ultimate goal is the *"increase of spiritual perception,"* which is, in essence, *unlimited*. This means that plenty of room remains for future researchers to contribute; but only after first completing their *Advanced Training* regarding the parts of our *"Map"* that are *already* researched, well-plotted, effective in application, and thus published.

A *Seeker* could complete *A.T. Manual #3*, and then move on directly to *Level-8* with *A.T. Manual #5* (*"Entities & Fragments"*). If, however, a *Seeker* doesn't have enough *"reality"* on that *Level-8* material—as in, it

doesn't seem *"real"* enough to them—
then some time studying *A.T. Manual #4*
(*"Implanted Universes"*) may be of benefit.
The covert purpose of introducing *"Implant Platforms #1-18"* *(AT#3)* and the
"IPU Platforms" *(AT#4)* at *Level-7,* is really
to make *"Entities & Fragments"* *(AT#5)*
more accessible.

To apply *upper-level Systemology*, an *advanced Seeker* must follow the prescribed
outline of instruction that is now available for the first time to the public as the
"Keys to the Kingdom" series.

*Advanced Manuals should be studied in the
sequential order in which they are numbered.*

A.T. MANUAL #8
ADVANCING
SYSTEMOLOGY

Keep these prerequisite materials accessible:
PC Lesson-1 to 16; Processing-Levels 0 to 6
AT Manual #1, "The Secret of Universes"
AT Manual #2, "Games, Goals & Purposes"
AT Manual #3, "The Jewel of Knowledge"
AT Manual #4, "Implanted Universes"
AT Manual #5, "Entities & Fragments"
AT Manual #6, "Spiritual Perception"
AT Manual #7, "Mastering Ascension"

NEW STANDARD SYSTEMOLOGY
–A New Dawn of Crystal Clarity–

This is the final training volume of *Systemology Level-8* and the entry-point to the *Infinity Grade* by which one might attain *certainty-of-Beingness* as an *Ascended Master* of *this Physical Universe*. This manual presents qualifying experimental *Wizard-Level 4* to 7 material. Use of this manual also requires applying *systematic processing* as a *research-action*, which will be explained throughout the text.

We are now reaching an end-cycle on this instructional communication—part of which includes a concise clarification of terms regarding the *levels* and *gradients* of material that have brought us this far. In brief—the *New Standard Systemology* used by the *Systemology Society* is represented with:

<u>Fundamentals of Systemology</u>
(Basic Course – *6 Lessons*)

<u>The Pathway to Ascension</u>
Processing-Levels 0 to 6
(Professional Course – *16 Lessons*)

<u>Keys to the Kingdom</u>
Processing-Levels 7 to 8
Wizard-Levels/Infinity-Grade
(Advanced Training – *8 Manuals*)
(Training Supplements – *3 Manuals*)

All *Systemology* publications not included in the list (above) are considered part of the *Systemology Core Research Library*—retained for additional *Pilot Training* and posterity as a detailed chronicle of the developments leading up to this newly refined *standard*. For the *Systemology Society*: the indicated *processing-levels* are treated *independent* of any *Mardukite Academy "Grade"* classification.

The *Mardukite Academy* provides *Systemology* instruction in addition to many other subjects—it has many other "gradients" to reflect that. From an *Academy* viewpoint: *"The Pathway to Ascension"* is *Grade-VI*; and *"Keys to the Kingdom"* represents *Grade-VII*. The only real parallel is the concept of an *"Infinity Grade"* for *8*.

Mardukite Esoteric Research Library
(Subject: Systemology – 16 Volumes)

Liber-8 : *Keys to the Kingdom: Vol. II*
Liber-7 : *Keys to the Kingdom: Vol. I*
Liber-6 (5B) : *Pathway/Ascension: Vol. II*
Liber-5 (5A) : *Pathway/Ascension: Vol. I*
Liber-4 : *Systemology: Backtrack*
Liber-180 : *Systemology-180*
Liber-3 (3E) : *The Way of the Wizard*
Liber-3D : *Imaginomicon*
Liber-2D : *Metahuman Destinations: Vol. II*
Liber-2C : *Metahuman Destinations: Vol. I*
Liber-2B : *Crystal Clear*
Liber-One : *Tablets of Destiny Revelation*
Liber-S1Z : *The Power of Zu (Lectures)*
Liber-S1X : *Systemology: Original Thesis*
Liber-S1W : *The Way Into The Future*
Liber-S1A : *Fundamentals of Systemology*

SYSTEMOLOGY–INFINITY

Effectively advancing *Systemology* research has specific requirements. Although the target-goal is always to develop a stable standard for *defragmenting* with certainty, the means by which this data is achieved is not always a very "therapeutic" activity—often "stirring things up" (*resurfacing*) in order to document them, without always having a safety-net. Fortunately, we have *now* reached a level of refinement to our research-methods (communicated in this manual) that will help a *Seeker* avoid the same *pitfalls* of our earlier efforts.

To make "advancements" in any subject requires an actual understanding of the subject you're trying to advance; *e.g. Systemology*. For our purposes, in addition to the *New Standard* courses, this might include examining all of the *Systemology Core Research Volumes*.

To push forth in a subject such as this really requires a strong dedication and passion to the pursuit of *Spiritual Ascension* and accessing the *Magic Kingdom*—which is, of course, the *Holy Grail* we have been after.

An advanced researcher needs to have handled their "*own case*"—or at least be able to get "*exterior to*" it—and also be able to see beyond any "mundane goal" attached to this work, such as fame or fortune. More than just "reading" the books, or "intellectually knowing" the material, a *systemologists* should be able to *apply* the spiritual technology to their lives, using the entire *Universe* as their "*laboratory.*"

Although there are obviously "unique" aspects of one's personal *Backtrack* that require "cleaning up," the target-focus of our *New Standard Systemology* are those major elements and specific *incidents* that are more "common" to all cases of the *earthbound "Human Condition"* — and particularly critical to keeping an *Alpha-Spirit "in"* that *condition*. Such data is easier to "test" and also support "systematically" with any certainty.

Most of our research is systematically developed utilizing *Biofeedback-Devices*. This provides greater accuracy when conducting *"Assessments"* (with existing *data-lists*) and *"Listing-Actions"* (to find data; to find a *correct item*). In most cases, this means *Solo-Piloting* with a *GSR-Meter*; or sometimes *Co-Piloting* with an experienced research assistant.

Even when something just "seems right" (or "clicks into place"), to be a *systematic research-action* requires checking/verifying if "what seems right" actually prompts *Meter-reads*. For example: is it a *charged* *"item-line"* of a *Platform*, or does it just "sound good." Just like when a *Seeker* first *"contacts"* an *incident* with their *Awareness*, sometimes this work requires

30

a bit of "feeling around" until something *registers* definitively.

The most important part of the *research-action* is: *Spotting "What Is"* — or realizing a lot of "*It is __ ,*" without a lot of questions (unknowns), other associations, and freewheeling thought. "*Spot 'What Is'*" with certainty, rather than focusing on what is still out of view, blocked, or heavily *fragmented*. If something is hidden, but not currently *restimulated*, approach it from angles where you have certainty.

When dealing with uncharted areas — particularly concerning *heavy incidents* and *Implant-Platforms* — there are several common ways mistakes can be made, including: missing *reads* (and *items*); putting *items* out-of-sequence; putting in *items* that aren't supposed to be there; and attributing *reading-items* to one part of an *incident*, when they really apply somewhere else, or even to a completely different *incident* or *Platform*.

Mistakes affect a researcher, just as they do a *Seeker*. When *turbulent charge* or *fragmentation* is missed or "flown by" without handling it, or a *Seeker runs* the "wrong" *item*, their case does not improve. Worse than that, one might become quite ill, or get feelings of "overwhelm" and "invalidation" that stalls or hinders progress. Technically *all systemologists* are "researchers" of their own *Backtrack*; but we don't directly encourage taking a "plunge" into unknown depths until certainty is had on what *is* known and accessible.

When hitting a research-block, or a point where a specific *item* just can't be reached, it is often a good idea to take a short break and let things cool down. You can leave your *session* set up and come back to it. You *don't* want to be sitting in *session*, repeatedly chanting *"What is it!?*

What is it!?" to yourself. *Research-actions* can cause *attention* to get *fixed*, frustrations can inhibit clarity, and underlying *restimulation* from unrecognized sources can affect progress. Make sure to check your "preventative fundamentals" at the start of each session.

To fully charge ahead *Self-honestly*, one must be *willing to be wrong*, while still maintaining cautious optimism and tolerance for confusion. Researching with a *GSR-Meter* requires *"unbiased objectivity"* —rather than trying to "steer" results to validate some preferred (personal) theory, *&tc.* And like any other *scientific research*: discoveries must be communicable and demonstrable to others; its methods should be able to be repeated by others—and hence our emphasis on that which is "common" to others, and *registers* as such.

To be a part of this progressive movement requires a *willingness to share know-*

ledge that will *help*, not *entrap*, your fellow *Seekers*. This means when these "*trap-mechanisms*" are discovered, they are shared with others so they can *realize* things as they are.

This knowledge is really only dangerous when it is kept secret, used for the personal gain of a few, or further control of the population, rather than as a means of *spiritual liberation*.

We have been faithfully honest in our relay of the *upper-level* work—where an *item* may be wrong, or a *Goal* is out-of-sequence; these things, when already sensed, have been indicated in the text. Areas that require additional details or data refinement are plainly noted. This is not a shortcoming on our part—for we have already advanced this material to a *New Standard* that has never been reached in the "*New Thought*" before. But the time has come to push this out from the shadows, making it available for other *Seekers* of the *Grail.*

Our *Systemology* is still relatively *"young"* compared to what can evolve from it. And an *Ascension "out"* of *this Universe* is not its only application. If more individuals became *"Seekers,"* we might just be able to *realize* a *"heaven-on-earth"* right where we are. At the very least, we can complete this *Map* for one another, and meet up again in the *Magic Kingdom*, once we've resolved all of our "stuff" down here.

Rather than spend a lot of time on theoretical philosophy, this manual will focus on *upper-level* areas that a *Seeker* will already be familiar with from previous manuals and lessons, but of which are still worthy of greater expansion and refinement. They are all developed enough to present here as launch-points for reaching further; and they all reflect critical points that remain unhandled, at least in part.

THE JEWEL OF KNOWLEDGE
(*Experimental Research*)

[The basic description and background information for *The Jewel of Knowledge* is found in "*The Secret of Universes*" (*AT#1*). This is supplemented by information concerning *False Jewels* in "*The Jewel of Knowledge*" (*AT#3*). The data provided in this current section is incomplete; therefore not included in former manuals.]

The Jewel, in any of its forms, is of popular interest among *A.T. Systemologists* and researchers. The "original" *Jewel of Knowledge* is not necessarily difficult to "*contact*," but it is particularly challenging to fully *process-out* when *perceptions* are heavily *fragmented*. It remains the most "obscure" of all incidents that an *Alpha-Spirit* has experienced.

The *original Jewel of Knowledge* is incredibly (and deceptively) basic—almost simpleminded. It would probably have little effect on an "experienced" *Alpha-Spirit*; but for an *innocent being* (with no former "*conception of existence*") freshly separated from the *Infinite*, it was sufficiently powerful in laying in the pattern of reality that is accounted for in *AT#1*.

When "scouting" for *experimental data*, it sometimes requires "feeling around" a bit, or "scanning through" what is known with certainty—and then seeing if any *perceptions*, or even vague impressions, occur. For example: "*they probably told us about how to perceive things.*" This is then checked with *Biofeedback* to see if anything *registers*. Once something is giving definitive *Meter-reads*, it is possible to check other things about it. Then, with more *certainties* to "*scan*" over, more details can emerge.

It is important to note that *intensive research-phases* were once critically necessary for producing material such as "*The Secret of Universes*" (*AT#1*)—or uncovering the nature of a particular *incident*. However, the initial *research-actions*, themselves, undertaken by various pioneers contributing to this work, seldom provided actual *gain* or personal *progress*. Any *relief* only seemed to occur after a particular *process* or *Platform* was at least 99% correct and fully developed for *systematic application*.

GSR-Meter assessments were used to generate most of the additional *experimental data* included here. Even the material here has only been partially *processed-out* by our researchers—which still leaves us with only a partial view of the whole picture. Only some of the *facet-chambers* of the original *Jewel of Knowledge* have been explored directly—leaving much missing-data to still recover. However, there is still much given here.

1. First Split-Viewpoint

Data: You see a *line* and feel as though there is more out of sight. You keep shifting around and seeing different *lines*. There is a sense that there is something greater present here, but you only see one *line* of it at a time. You decide that if you can view two different *lines* simultaneously, that you might *Know* something. So you hold your *attention* on one line, while trying to look at another line, which splits your *viewpoint*.

Now you see through two different *viewpoints*; and by holding them simultaneously, you are able to perceive a "plane" (*planar surface*). Usually it resembles a "square"; but if you shift your *viewpoints* around, it appears otherwise, such as a "triangle." You still feel like there is *more* to *Know*. So, you steady your *attention* on the "plane" while pulling yourself back to "see more"—which splits another *viewpoint* and allows you to see a *three-dimensional* object; usually a "cube"; but again, as you shift your *viewpoints*, you can see that you are looking at different shapes.

The same splitting and perception occurs for *4-D* and *5-D space/objects*; and you "feel good" about this. The *object* being displayed is really a *5-D* object with a *6-D* thickness. When you try splitting further into *six*, the *object* holds steady, and you see some additional thickness to it, but nothing really more. In fact, it starts to appear somewhat ghostly and unreal from that view, which makes you "feel sad" about it.

So, you decide to forget about the *sixth-dimension* and *pretend* the object is *real* enough from before. You go back to admiring it how it was when you "felt good" about it; and decide there is nothing more to *Know*. That's when the experience of this *facet-chamber* ends, and you shift into the next *facet* in the sequence.

2. Need For Agreement

Data: Experience of the next *facet* begins with only a *white-nothingness* or *white-void*. You reach your *Awareness* for something to see but there is nothing. Eventually, you sense the presence of another *being*. You shift your *attention* around until you are able to feel the nearness of one of their *viewpoints*. When you shift your own *viewpoint* to their *viewpoint*, you are able to perceive a *curved-line*.

At first you only see the *curved-line*, but you get a sense that the other *being* is looking at a full *5-D object*. You split your *viewpoint* into *five* to try and see it, but you still only perceive a *curved-line*. You realize that this is because only *one* of your *viewpoints* is matching theirs. When you match all *five viewpoints* to theirs, a *5-*

D sphere appears, and you "feel good" about this because it is interesting and permits something greater to *have* a perception of.

You experiment by shifting a *viewpoint* off of theirs, and this causes the *sphere* to "lose" a *dimension* and seem more hollow, which gives a sense of less "*havingness*" and "*loss*" — and makes you "feel bad" about it. When you shift your *viewpoint* back into *agreement* with the *other being*, you "feel better" about it — and decide that *agreement* is a necessary factor. [Then you shift to the *next facet*.]

3. Duplicating Others

Data: You sense another *being*. They manifest/create a "*point*" and extend a *line* from that *point*; then encourage you to do the same. When you eventually do this, you have a *line*. But, since you don't locate it within the same *Space* as theirs, you lose track of their *line* while making yours. After realizing this, you decide to manifest/create your *line* in the same *Space* as theirs, and now you *have* two *lines* to perceive.

Eventually, the other *being* splits their viewpoints to make a square (plane) and invites you to do the same. This is repeated with *3-D* and *4-D cubes*. Each time you get a sense of increased "*havingness*" by making these more interesting objects in agreement with another's creation. You realize the need for following directions and duplicating others.

4. Need For Games

Data: This *facet-chamber* is experienced within a *thirteen-dimensional space*. There are many "*cubes*" with white and black sides. They resemble modern "*dice*" in that the "quantities" shown on their faces/sides are represented by "dots" rather than "symbols." Moving them around at random is uninteresting. Eventually, you find that sorting and arranging them in "sequences" (*&tc.*) is far more interesting and fun.

5. Need For Opponents

Data: There are a series of cubes (as in FACET 4); but this time there are two sets (one white and one black) and a sense that there is another *being* present. The two sets are not identical and the quantities represented on their faces are "random" (non-sequential, with missing numbers). You each take a set and have a "race" to see who can get them in "order" first. You find this more interesting and fun than arranging them alone.

6. Need To Ensure An Opponent

Data: Similar to FACET 5; but when the opponent "weakens," the game becomes less fun. So you encourage and try to help them.

7. Need To Create An Opponent

Data: Set up like earlier *facets*; but this time there is no opponent. You decide to *divide*—and part of you serves to act as the opponent. You realize the necessity of this in order to have a *game*.

8. Need For Barriers

Data: There is a *7-D cube* with variously-shaped holes and slots. There are different *objects* around that can be fitted into them. You can perceive another *being* doing this and it looks interesting. When it's your turn, the *objects* just drift through the *cube-walls* and each other, and it's not very fun or challenging. You decide that it is only fun when you make the *objects* solid and the *walls* more solid to block things.

9. Encouraging Agreement

Data: You perceive there are four other *beings* in the space. You each share in manifesting/creating a *5-D cube.* This provides a "pleasant feeling" (*havingness*). When one of the others goes out-of-agreement, the *cube* goes hollow. Eventually, some of the others encourage them to get back into-agreement and the *cube* is solid again and "nicer."

Then it happens again where someone goes out-of-agreement, and this time you encourage them to come back into-agreement (and the *cube* is solid again).

Then you decide to go out-of-agreement and leave the "group" and can only see a *line*. You sense the encouragement of others to come back into-agreement (and the *cube* is solid again). Then you all admire the solid *cube* for a while and it is "pleasant." You decide it is necessary to encourage the agreement of others.

10. Need To Agree On Barriers

Data: Similar to FACET 8; but the large object is a *5-D pyramid,* and there are many other *beings* playing, all racing to put their *objects* into the *holes* and *slots*. But everything starts quite transparent and isn't much fun. So, you learn how to make each other's *objects* more solid in order to *have* a *game*.

11. Need To Enforce Agreement

Data: This occurs in a *many-dimensional* space. There are specifically *14* dimensions that are not properly aligned (in right-angles to each other) and *14* different *beings* present. Each different *being* is manifesting/creating a *"dimension point"* that is *anchoring* each single dimensional-space. You are each trying to align two *4-D objects* and get them onto the same axis until everyone can get into-agreement on dimensional-space.

No one is making any progress. You finally *agree* with another to share your *anchor-points*. Now the two of you have more in alignment than the others who insist on being individualistic. You, and the other one agreeing with you, decide to *Implant* each of the others with the intention to "go into-agreement." This is accomplished by taking a *being* and "holding" them in the *object* until they *choose to agree* with it.

Since you are "blocking" their *dimension-points* (perceptions) while you do this, they eventually agree. And since your "side" always outnumbers any individual, you never fail in this task. In fact, it gets much easier as more are added to the group. When everyone is in agreement, the *spatial-dimensions collapse* into a *single reality-frequency* that is pleasing to everyone. And from this, you see the necessity of forcing others into-agreement.

12. Sensation

Data: You see a *4-D object* in front of you. It has *13* different *3-D "sides"*—each of which is a *3-D object* (a *square-based pyramid*). *Ten* of the *3-D pyramids* are solid and *three* are hollow. You receive an *intention/impression* that this is "your form" and you sense an encouragement in becoming it. So, you *choose to be the object* (the *multi-pyramid form*) just to see what happens.

Then, a *4-D energy-beam* comes in and

starts bouncing in and out of your new form. It enters via a *hollow pyramid* and then ricochets off the *solid pyramids* before going out one of the *hollow* ones. Since there are only *three hollow pyramids*, the activity of the *energy-beam* seems unbalanced and you get a sense of incompleteness.

Then another *being* with a similar form as yours is present. The two of you align your *hollow* areas, share the *energy-beams* with one another; and everything is pleasant, harmonic, and you get the sense of this being *"pleasure."* Then the other *being* turns away from you (out-of-alignment), and the *energy-beams* are now all jagged and disorganized. It is not enjoyable, and you get the impression that this is *"pain."*

13. Pleasure Is At Other's Expense

Data: You follow the *being* from the previous *facet* into this chamber, where you find yourselves among a total of *14 beings* all using the "*multi-pyramid bodies.*" There are *energy-beams* bouncing all around the *Space*, and you participate in the exchange of them—but the *beams* are out-of-alignment (feel mildly unpleasant).

Two of the *beings* get into good alignment with each other and begin to experience "*pleasure*" (as described in FACET 12. But this throws everyone else's *beams* into a worse alignment—and you feel "*pain.*" So, everyone pushes the *two* out-of-alignment with each other.

Then you have the chance to be in-alignment with another, and do so. It is "*pleasant,*" but you notice that everyone else is in "*pain*" again, so you allow them to push you apart. Everyone, including yourself, goes back to feeling only the "*mildly unpleasant*" pattern (as in the beginning).

14. Need For Rules
Data: You watch *three beings* operating in a *7-D space.* *Two* of them create an elabor-

ate *game* with what appears to be various spirals, rods, cones, energies, and balls bouncing around. You can see that they are interested and enjoying their *game*.

Then the *third being* joins them and wants to play too. But they don't know the *rules* of the *game*, so they invent their own and start playing differently. The first *two* get frustrated and start modifying the *rules* in order to accommodate the new player, but the *game* becomes too chaotic and falls apart. The players break off and examine the results and are "unhappy."

They get back together again; but this time they define clear *rules* for each of the aspects of the *game*, and even *create* something that puts the *rules on display*. But it does more than display them; it *Implants* them. So, when a *fourth being* arrives, they are *Implanted* with the *rules* before they are allowed to *play*. Now things can proceed well and everyone is mostly "satisfied" with the results.

When it comes time for you to come and join the *game*, you have already witnessed the *"need for rules,"* and so you *agree to being Implanted* for the sake of sharing in the *game*.

15. Need For Players

Data: A *"multi-dimensional sphere"* is being bounced back and forth between two "teams" (comprised of maybe *eight beings* on each side). Participating in the *game* provides a *"pleasant"* sensation. Then, one of the other players wanders off and the *game* is a little less fun. This causes more to wander off, and there is eventually no one else left but you. For a while, you sit alone and bored.

Then another group arrives and you all play together. When one of the players tries to leave, the others "hold" them and "force" them back into the *game*. Then the *game* remains *"pleasant."* When you have fully realized a necessity to force others to remain in a game, you shift to the *next facet*.

Other facet-chambers requiring research:

16. Need For Duplication
17. Need For Imperfect Duplication
18. Need For Persistence
19. Need For Admiration
20. Need For Acknowledgment
21. Need To Divide
22. Only One Will Survive (Win)
23. {the idea that if two terminals connect to communicate, one will be submissive and the other will be dominant}
24. {the idea that if you communicate too freely, you will connect to terminals that will dominate you}

THE FALSE JEWEL OF KNOWLEDGE
(*Experimental Research*)

Although there have been many *False Jewels* (such as *Entry-Into-This-Universe*), this *Implant* appears relatively early on the *Backtrack*—between the "*Games Univ-*

erse" and the "Symbols Universe" — and is considered the earliest "False Jewel."

By the point of this *incident*, an *Alpha-Spirit* had already experienced the *Implant Penalty-Universes* (IPU) and maintained some *fragmented considerations* from the *Games Universe*. But visibly, this only affected what we tended to *create* (*manifest*) or *dramatize*. There was no conception that: to *Implant* caused *fragmentation* that affected us as *beings*. The intention was to simply suppress or limit the interactions in a *Shared-Reality*; but our *Actualized Awareness* and *spiritual abilities* were being *fragmented* in the process.

During the phase of existence that this *Implant* occurred, an *Alpha-Spirit* was still unaffected by *force* or any *energy* directly. Also, we had not yet experienced a heavy "*Splitter-Incident*" that would *actually divide* our *Awareness* into "*split-viewpoints*" (that could individually get *Implanted* without our being conscious of it). At this stage, we were still able to *"collect ourselves"* after an *Implanting-Incident*; such as seems to have been the case after the original IPU experiences. But an individual could still be tricked into limiting themselves.

Although the original *Jewel* had been lost to a fog of *fragmented-time*, it was still treated with a religious-like veneration. Pale *facsimiles* of it were used to make IPU more impactful; but there was no specific emphasis on using them for *Implanting* at that time. Here, the *re-creation* or *facsimile* of *The Jewel* is intentionally used to install *false data* and *fragmented reasoning*—therefore, we refer to it as the *earliest "False Jewel."* Of course, all *Implants* install *"false data,"* but here we concentrate on one *incident* where that is *the* focus.

This *False Jewel* is awarded as a *"prize"* for winning some *game*. The *game* is actually designed for the individual to *"win,"* but they get a sense of earning something valuable. The *Implant* also impresses the individual to trick others into being victim to the *False Jewel* (by promoting how "wonderful" it is to have).

At the start of the *Implant*: *The False Jewel* moves *"into"* the individual's *"center of Beingness."* *The Jewel* *"flashes"* with each *item*. It is a kind of *radioactive-light* (that accompanies an *electric-crackle*) and spreads completely throughout the individual. The *Platform* begins with a series of *command-items* (all of which are included below).

In *3-D perception*, *The Jewel* resembles a *"diamond"*—an *eight-sided solid*, or *two pyramids* (one pointing up; one pointing down) sharing a base. As a *"higher-dimensional construct,"* it actually has *64 sides* or *"facets."*

The second part of the incident uses *graphic imagery (symbolism)* to install *64 fragmented agreements* (that follow the *bas-*

ic IPU-*sequence*). *The Jewel* "turns" to present *one* of its *64* different "*facets.*" During this part, the "*radioactive flashes*" emit a brief "*motion picture*" (rather than a "*command-line*").

Each of the *64 facets* present a different "*motion picture*" that is only loosely connected to the literal IPU and seldom includes any of the major "*terminals.*" Each of these *facets* relay a "basic truth" about existence—but, of course, it is all *fragmented false-data* (*lies*).

Each "*motion picture*" is sensed as a "heavy flow"—but it is not so much an "energy" as it is an *internally generated* sense of "overwhelm" or "dread" at the sudden *flash-realization* of the (false) truth. This produces an intensely receptive "haze" (or "daze") of *Awareness*. Such "*flash-insights*" might otherwise be "shrugged off" and ignored with a few moments of *analytic thought*; but in this particular state of "shock," we *agree* that we *believe* them.

After receiving the "(*false*)-*truth*" from a *facet*: we *agree* to it; then *The Jewel* gets us to *agree-to-forget* it—and hide that *agreement* (with the *false-truth*) from ourselves —because the "truth is too terrible" and would drive us "insane" if we *knew, &tc. The Jewel* then turns to its next *facet* and emits the next *motion-picture* and *false-truth*. The information from one "truth" tends to contradict another; but since each one is forgotten before the next, this doesn't seem to get noticed during the *incident*.

This is a particularly significant area of advanced research, because the *Platform* for this "original" *False Jewel* was likely copied and reused (or added to) many times in subsequent *Universes* on the *Backtrack*. "Spotting" the top of the original *False Jewel* (*Platform*) aids in releasing "Control Entities" (C.E.) [*AT#5*], so there is certainly some validity to what we have already uncovered. However, the research on the *64 facets* is still incomplete.

(ORIGINAL) FALSE JEWEL PLATFORM

A. {*Winning the game.*}

B. {*Being given The Jewel and agreeing to accept it.*}

C. {*The Jewel flows into you.*}

D. {*The Jewel flashes in the center of your being on each of the following command-items.*}

1. TO ACCEPT THE JEWEL IS NATIVE STATE
2. TO ACCEPT THE JEWEL IS TO BE THE STATIC (ALPHA)
3. TO ACCEPT THE JEWEL IS TO FULFILL THE URGE FOR SOMETHINGNESS
4. THE JEWEL IS THE BASIS FOR ALL URGES
5. THE JEWEL IS THE BASIS FOR ALL RELIEF

6. THE JEWEL IS THE ONLY REASON WHY
7. THE JEWEL IS THE BASIS FOR ALL ACTION
8. IN THE BEGINNING, NOW, AND FOREVER, IS THE DECISION; AND THE DECISION IS TO ACCEPT THE JEWEL
9. THE JEWEL CONTAINS ALL REAL DECISIONS
10. THE JEWEL CONTAINS ALL REAL POSTULATES
11. THE JEWEL CONTAINS ALL REAL AGREEMENTS
12. THE JEWEL IS THE ONLY SOURCE OF TIME
13. THE JEWEL IS THE ONLY SOURCE OF SPACE
14. THE JEWEL IS THE ONLY SOURCE OF ENERGY
15. THE JEWEL IS THE ONLY SOURCE OF MATTER
16. THE JEWEL CONTAINS ALL LOVE
17. THE JEWEL CONTAINS ALL EMOTION

18. THE JEWEL CONTAINS ALL THOUGHT
19. THE JEWEL CONTAINS ALL EFFORT
20. THE JEWEL CONTAINS ALL KNOWLEDGE
21. THE JEWEL CONTAINS ALL UNDERSTANDING
22. THE JEWEL IS THE SOURCE OF ALL REALITY
23. THE JEWEL IS THE SOURCE OF ALL MEANING
24. THE JEWEL IS THE SOURCE OF ALL TRUTH
25. THE JEWEL IS THE SOURCE OF ALL BEAUTY
26. THE JEWEL IS THE SOURCE OF ALL VALUE
27. THE JEWEL IS THE SOURCE OF ALL HAVING(NESS)
28. THE JEWEL IS THE SOURCE OF ALL EXISTENCE
29. THE JEWEL IS THE SOURCE OF ALL ENLIGHTENMENT
30. TO ACCEPT THE JEWEL IS TO REACH TOTAL KNOWINGNESS

31. TO ACCEPT THE JEWEL IS TO LEARN THE HIDDEN MEANINGS BEHIND ALL EXISTENCE
32. TO ACCEPT THE JEWEL IS TO KNOW THE TRUE REASON FOR EVERYTHING

E. {*The Jewel turns to its first facet. Motion-picture. False-data. Agreements.*}

"FALSE JEWEL" FRAGMENTED-DATA

Each *facet* of *The Jewel* presents *false-data* using elements of one of the IPU *and* its "inversion" (a negative quality or opposition for each IPU). Some of the existing research on this *false-data* is listed below along with its corresponding IPU. [The entire subject of IPU is still under development and refinement.]

One challenge of this research concerns how many times a *"False Jewel"* has been used with different content. Our target-data here pertained to the *Original "False Jewel."* When other related data was found, but determined to apply only to a *later* (more recent) version of the "*False Jewel*," it is indicated as such.

[*Advisement*: the *false-data* discovered and provided here IS *false-data*. It sometimes sounds "right" to make it more acceptable—and has become a part of many basic *reality-agreements*. But it is not, itself, truth. It is full of half-truths, inaccurate evaluations, and the resulting considerations. The research discoveries are included here for *processing-out*; not to be mistaken as real "wisdom." *The Jewel*, in all of its forms, always provides "*False Enlightenment*"—but it is also the *only* "*enlightenment*" that most individuals ever find.]

[The "*Hellfire Incident Location*" is only used *later* in this manual. It is given here to avoid having to print the *Goals-list* twice in the same volume.]

[16. **CREATION** (*Arc 8*)]

1. "TO CREATE" {*statue*}

 (–) "TO DESTROY" {*devil statue*}

False-Data: 'God' created everything and we just keep messing it up. So you agree that you must never create or destroy anything because it's all really God's *Universe*, not yours.

[*Hellfire Inc. (loc)*—St. John, Canada]

2. "TO CAUSE" {*old man god*}

 (–) "TO PUT AT EFFECT" {*devil*}

False-Data: When you manifest/create/cause things, they cease to be under your control. So you agree that it is dangerous to manifest anything. —*Later*: If you could manifest real things in this *Universe*, the ability would go out of control; and you'd manifest things that you are afraid of, which would attack you. So you agree to keep your manifestations from becoming real.

[*Hellfire Inc. (loc)*—Rome]

3. "TO DUPLICATE" {*computer*}

(or "TO INTENSIFY")

(–) "TO UNMANIFEST" {*black computer*}

(or "TO DRAIN") {*black vortex*}

False-Data: When you fight back against something, it is intensified by your efforts to resist it. So you agree not to fight back.

—*Later*: If you think of something, it will get stronger and gain power over you. So you agree not to think about anything outside of normal reality.

[*Hellfire Inc. (loc)*—Washington, DC]

4. "TO IMAGINE" {*cartoon*}

(–) "TO DISILLUSION" {*vampyre*}

False-Data: There are horrific things beyond the *third-dimension* that don't want you to see them, and will attack you if you do. So you agree not to *imagine* anything beyond the *third-dimension*.

—*Later*: If your *imagination* goes out-of-control, you will *imagine* your worst fears. So you agree not to *imagine* anything.

[*Hellfire Inc. (loc)*—Florida or Brazil]

[15. **KNOWINGNESS** (*Arc 7*)]

 5. "TO KNOW" {*2-headed dodo*}

  (–) "TO MISLEAD" {*gorilla-people*}

False-Data: When you knew the real truth, you chose to forget it for good reasons. So you agree not to try to know the real truth.

—*Later*: If the people knew the truth, it would destroy them. So you agree that you must prevent any attempts to reveal the truth.

 [*Hellfire Inc. (loc)*—S. Argentina]

 6. "TO UNDERSTAND" {*chipmunk*}

  (–) "TO MISUNDERSTAND" {*disabled*}

False-Data: If something *could* be understood, you *would* understand it *already*. The only things worth understanding belong to 'God' and are not to be understood by you. So you agree not to try and understand anything because it would be a worthless effort.

 [*Hellfire Inc. (loc)*—Vermont]

 7. "TO ABSORB" {*epic hero*}

(–) "TO DISCARD" {*amazonian*}
False-Data: Beings (entities) are the coin (currency) of the *Universe*; and you can only gain strength and power by absorbing them.

[*Hellfire Inc. (loc)*—Mt. Olympus]

8. "TO LEARN" {*gnome*}
   (–) "TO FORGET" {*troll*}
False-Data: If you learned the truth, it would destroy the *Game*. So you agree to forget this (*The Jewel*) forever.

[*Hellfire Inc. (loc)*—Heidelberg, Germany]

[14. **GAMES** (*Arc 6*)]

9. "TO PLAY" {*child*}
   (–) "TO FOOL" {*joker*}
False-Data: Life is only a *game* and you exist here only as a playing-piece. So you agree that it doesn't matter what you do, or what happens, since there is no higher purpose anyway.
—*Later*: We are all one, so that when you lose to someone else, you have really

won, because you are them too. So you agree to lose often, to help yourself win elsewhere.

[*Hellfire Inc. (loc)*—Shanghai, China]

10. "TO COMPETE" {*coach*}
   (–) "TO CHEAT" {*skeleton*}

False-Data: If people compete, only one can win, and many must lose. So you agree to lose the majority of the time.

—*Later*: If you were strong, you would be selfish and evil forever. So you agree to stay weak.

[*Hellfire Inc. (loc)*—Toronto, Canada]

11. "TO MANIPULATE" {*penguin banker*}
   (–) "TO RUIN" {*dragon*}

False-Data: The 'Fates' secretly manipulate your behavior, and you can't do anything about it. So you agree not to take responsibility for anything, because none of it is your fault.

—*Later*: There are evil people who would manipulate society for their own gain and bring harm to others. So you agree to block anyone who tries to manipulate society.

[*Hellfire Inc. (loc)*—Zurich, Switzerland]

12. "TO EXCHANGE" {*spirit-broker*}

(–) "TO STEAL" {*raccoon*}

False-Data: You gave up your right to disagree in exchange for the chance to 'play' in this *Game.* So you agree not to disagree with the 'rules' of the *Universe.*

—*Later*: You promised 'God' service in exchange for life. So you agree to serve 'God' always and obey the rules of 'his' *Universe* (and not question anything).

[*Hellfire Inc. (loc)*—Hong Kong, China]

[13. **CHANGE** (*Arc 5*)]

13. "TO SHAPE" {*clay people*}

(–) "TO DISTORT" {*walrus*}

False-Data: You were shaped (made/created) from the postulates of others. So you agree that other's postulates should affect you.

[*Hellfire Inc. (loc)*—Crete, Greece]

14. "TO CHANGE" {*magician*}

   (–) "TO IMPLODE" {*sorceress*}

False-Data: This *Universe* is a constructed picture, and you are only a figure painted in it by the 'Master-Painter'—moving and acting as is needed to compose the painting. So you agree that you can affect nothing, and cannot change (you must be as you are).

   [*Hellfire Inc. (loc)*—Tunisia, N. Africa]

15. "TO COMBINE" {*conjoined twins*}

   (–) "TO FRAGMENT" {*worms*}

False-Data: Reality can only be manifested/created or affected by group postulation. If you are alone, then you will have no *Universe*. So you agree to combine with other beings and stick to them.

   [*Hellfire Inc. (loc)*—Rangoon, Yangon]

16. "TO (BRING) ORDER" {*gorilla people*}

      (or "TO ALIGN") {*bear-people*}

   (–) "TO (BRING) CHAOS"

      (or "TO REVOLT") {*panther*}

False-Data: Our attempts to be individuals, and go our own way, brings us to a sorry state. So you agree to align with 'God' and follow 'his' desires, and put aside you own wants and needs.

[*Hellfire Inc. (loc)*—St. Petersburg, Russia]

[12. **REASON** (*Arc 4*)]

17. "TO REASON" {*clown*}

(–) "TO DISCOMBOBULATE" {*one-man band*}

False-Data: The real reason for existence is to feed your 'soul' to 'God'. So you agree to allow yourself to be eaten when the time comes.

[*Hellfire Inc. (loc)*—Manhattan, N.Y.]

18. "TO ORIENT" {*wire man*}

(–) "TO DISORIENT" {*spinning top*}

False-Data: If you were truly 'oriented', you would see that this is all a sham and an illusion and all your 'havingness' would be lost. So you agree to remain disoriented forever.

[*Hellfire Inc. (loc)*—Polar Orbit]

19. "TO GUIDE" {*pilot*}

   (–) "TO MISDIRECT" {*scarecrow*}

False-Data: You were once a god and supposed to guide everyone, but you failed and it's your fault that everyone is stuck here now. So you agree to remain here and suffer with everyone else because it's all your fault.

[*Hellfire Inc. (loc)*—Indianapolis]

20. "TO COMPUTE" {*toy bodies*}

   (–) "TO CONFUSE" {*zombie*}

False-Data: You must use a 'brain' to think and perceive. So you agree to be 'unconscious' whenever you are out of the 'body'.

[*Hellfire Inc. (loc)*—North Pole]

[11. CONSTRUCTION (*Arc 3*)]

21. "TO CONSTRUCT" {*beavers*}

   (–) "TO TEAR DOWN" {*wrecking crane*}

False-Data: Everything 'new' is constructed from the remains of older masses and energies. So you agree that nothing can be truly created or destroyed.

[*Hellfire Inc. (loc)*—Bangor, Maine]

22. "TO ENGINEER" {*lobsters*}
     (or "TO ARRANGE")
   (–) "TO UNSTABILIZE" {*goon*}
False-Data: The 'body' was engineered to be a 'spirit-trap' and you can't get out of it until you die. So you agree to accept death and to die as soon as possible to get out of the 'trap'.

[*Hellfire Inc. (loc)*—S. African lake]

23. "TO BUILD" {*snake people*}
   (–) "TO WRECK" {*raging bull*}
False-Data: Matter was built by many beings working in conjunction. So you agree that your postulates alone are not capable of affecting matter.

[*Hellfire Inc. (loc)*—In orbit; and Alaska]

24. "TO STRUCTURE" {*crystals*}
   (–) "TO SHATTER" {*bat-man*}
False-Data: The *Universe* is structured so that objects are 'real', and thoughts are

'unreal'. So you agree that your thoughts cannot really affect anything.

[*Hellfire Inc. (loc)*—Great Salt Lake, UT]

[10. **AESTHETICS** (*Arc 2*)]

25. "TO INVENT" {*worker gnomes*}
   (–) "TO DIVEST" {*troll*}

False-Data: You are the only real person and you invented everyone else. So you agree to divide and put out fragmented-pieces of yourself on everyone else to keep them (?) {manifested, under control, in a body..?}

[*Hellfire Inc. (loc)*—Bavaria (Germany)]

26. "TO ENHANCE" {*ghost people*}
   (–) "TO DEGRADE" {*demon*}
       (or "TO WORSEN")

False-Data: The *Universe* was created to 'teach' you a lesson that you desperately need (for enhancement). So you agree to go along with it, and try to learn from it, and not protest or rebel against what happens to you.

74

[*Hellfire Inc. (loc)* — Copenhagen, Denmark]

27. "TO INSPIRE" {*muses*}
  (–) "TO OCCLUDE" {*mesmerist*}
        (or "TO CONCEAL/BLOCK")
False-Data: Only 'divine inspiration' can bring about 'beauty' (aesthetic art). The whispered inspiration that artists and creators receive comes from 'God'. So you agree to 'listen' for it and obey any whispers (impressions) that appear in your 'mind', because they are 'divine inspiration'.

[*Hellfire Inc. (loc)* — Florence, Italy]

28. "TO BEAUTIFY" {*fairy godmother*}
  (–) "TO MAKE UGLY" {*old witch*}
False-Data: All 'beauty' comes from 'God'. So you agree that anything you create on your own must be ugly.

[*Hellfire Inc. (loc)* — Babylon]

[9. ETHICS (*Arc 1*)]

29. "TO PURIFY" {*fire people*}

(−) "TO PERVERT" {*satyr*}

False-Data: All your own 'desire' is impure and stems from some 'deep-seeded animal nature'. So you agree to suppress all urges, desires, and goals, in order to 'purify' your 'soul'.

[*Hellfire Inc. (loc)*—Lima, Peru]

30. "TO JUDGE" {*minotaur*}

(−) "TO DISAGREE" {*snake*}

False-Data: We are all in an *Implant* right now, and existence is just an *'item'*—so you agree that you cannot disagree with, or alter, reality because it's... {not there to be altered (?)}

[*Hellfire Inc. (loc)*—Crete, Greece]

31. "TO DEFEND" {*little green men*}

(−) "TO ATTACK" {*gorilla soldier*}

False-Data: The only real being is 'society'—which is 'God'. We are only 'cells' of its 'body'. So you agree to defend 'society' from {certain type?} individuals who work against it.

[*Hellfire Inc. (loc)*—Japan]

32. "TO STRENGTHEN" {*energy ball*}
      (or "TO PROTECT")
  (–) "TO HURT" {*silver ball*}
False-Data: There are 'higher-beings' ('celestial police', 'angels', *&tc.*) who are protecting you from extreme harm. So you agree to give them your loyalty and never question their methods.

  [*Hellfire Inc. (loc)*— (?)]

[8. **DIVINITY** (*Sphere 8*)]

33. "TO ENLIGHTEN" {*rabbit preacher*}
   (–) "TO OBSCURE" {*smog monster*}
False-Data: The real truth is so terrible or horrific that if you were to know it, it would you drive you insane. So you agree that you must forget it.

  [*Hellfire Inc. (loc)*—Libya or Jerusalem]

34. "TO CONVERT" {*fish man*}
   (–) "TO DISABUSE" {*jackal*}
False-Data: People will kill anyone that tries to help them. So you agree not to try to help others.

  [*Hellfire Inc. (loc)*—Jakarta, Indonesia]

35. "TO COMMUNE" {*feminine angel*}
    (or "TO CONNECT")
    (–) "TO DISCONNECT" {*spider-woman*}

False-Data: We are all fragmented-pieces of a Devil/Satan—a being that rebelled against 'God', looked at 'The Jewel of Knowledge' (which was forbidden), and was punished by being fragmented and sent here. So you agree that we all deserve to be punished and should suffer here complacently.

[*Hellfire Inc. (loc)*—Los Angeles, CA]

36. "TO WORSHIP" {*holy knights*}
    (–) "TO PROFANE" {*monk*}

False-Data: We were created for the sole purpose of worshiping 'God'—and that worship consists of taking on 'his' suffering. So you agree to devote yourself to suffering for 'God' and accept it without protest.

[*Hellfire Inc. (loc)*—England]

[7. **SPIRITUAL** (*Sphere 7*)]

37. "TO PREDICT" {*soothsayer*}

(or "TO PREDETERMINE")

(–) "TO RANDOMIZE" {*3-headed griffin*}

False-Data: The entire history (track) of the *Universe* was predetermined at its inception (creation). So you agree to follow the course laid out for you and not to try to change anything.

[*Hellfire Inc. (loc)*—Turkey]

38. "TO INFLUENCE" {*cupid/cherub*}

(–) "TO CORRUPT" {*hunchback*}

False-Data: When left uncontrolled, people will work against each other. So you agree to push fragmented-pieces of yourself onto others to influence them to work together.

[*Hellfire Inc. (loc)*—Jacksonville, FL]

39. "TO COLLECT" {*elves/fairies*}

(–) "TO REJECT" {*wolf-man*}

False-Data: We all sprang from the same 'eternal source' and must become 'one' again. So you agree to stick to other beings and try to merge with them.

[*Hellfire Inc. (loc)*—Bombay, India]

40. "TO EMBODY" {*satyr*}
     (or "TO PERMEATE")
  (–) "TO DISSOLVE" {*amoeba*}
False-Data: The 'divine light' permeates everything and is the only true source of energy. So you agree that you cannot (internally/personally) create any energy and must be dependent on an outside/external source.

[*Hellfire Inc. (loc)*—Catalina Island]

40X. "TO SOLIDIFY" {*satyr*}
  (–) "TO MAKE IT NOT-IS" {*invisible man*}
False-Data: All matter consists of decayed beings. So you agree that matter can affect you.

[6. **UNIVERSE** (*Sphere 6*)]

41. "TO DISCOVER" {*centaurs*}
  (–) "TO HIDE" {*slime monster*}
False-Data: This is the only *Universe* there is. So you agree that discovering anything

'outside' of this *Universe* must be a hallu-cination.

[*Hellfire Inc. (loc)*—New Zealand]

42. "TO LOCATE" {*leprechaun*}

 (–) "TO MISPLACE" {*cricket*}

False-Data: Each being has a unique 'loca-tion'—a 'viewpoint'—bestowed by 'God'. This locational viewpoint is where you do all your perceiving and thinking from. [Two separate locations would be two separate individuals.] So you agree that you cannot be in two places at once.

[*Hellfire Inc. (loc)*—In orbit (space-sta-tion)]

43. "TO GATHER" {*spacesuit body*}

 (–) "TO ABANDON" {*hobo/tramp*}

False-Data: Our 'souls' are all gathered up by 'God' when we die. So you agree to give up all 'Identity' when you lose the 'body'.

[*Hellfire Inc. (loc)*—Nepal, Asia]

44. "TO OWN" {*fox people*}

     (or "TO PERMEATE")

(–) "TO BURN DOWN" {*fire-people*}
False-Data: (?)
  [*Hellfire Inc. (loc)*—Rio de Jenero, Brazil]

[5. **LIFEFORMS** (*Sphere 5*)]

45. "TO GROW" {*genetic entity*}
  (–) "TO ROT" {*fungus creature*}
False-Data: (?)
  [*Hellfire Inc. (loc)*—Tahiti Island]

46. "TO LIVE" {*dinosaur*}
      (or "TO ENERGIZE") { ? }
  (–) "TO DIE" {*spectre*}
      (or "TO SHOCK") {*electric man*}
False-Data: The 'soul' can only be 'energized' by self-sacrifice. So you agree to sacrifice parts of yourself for the 'common good'.
  [*Hellfire Inc. (loc)*—the southern aurora]

47. "TO HEAL" {*tree man*}
  (–) "TO INFECT" {*germ colony*}
False-Data: (?)
  [*Hellfire Inc. (loc)*—Prague, Czech Rep.]

48. "TO ADAPT" {*thread man*}

(−) "TO PROTEST" {*snake*}
False-Data: (?)
  [*Hellfire Inc. (loc)*—Northern Siberia]

[4. **SOCIETY** (*Sphere 4*)]
 49. "TO ESTABLISH" {*3-eyed giants*}
   (−) "TO UNDERMINE" {*3-eyed robot*}
False-Data: 'Society' is a conscious entity
—individuals are only cells in that consciousness, and therefore unimportant.
So you agree that you must control others
for the sake of society.
  [*Hellfire Inc. (loc)*—Philadelphia, PA]
 50. "TO SHARE" {*dolphins*}
   (−) "TO POSSESS" {*sea monster*}
False-Data: A 'copy' is always less than the
'original'. We are all the result of a long
string of 'copies'. So you agree that you
will always be a 'flawed copy' without
the original's abilities.
[Some of this data might really apply to
another *facet* instead. (?)]
  [*Hellfire Inc. (loc)*—near Hawaii]

51. "TO CONTROL" {frog king}

  (–) "TO REBEL" {gargoyle}

False-Data: If people were left uncontrolled, everything would fall apart (be destroyed). So you agree that you must control others for their own good.

  [Hellfire Inc. (loc) — Caspian Sea]

52. "TO UNITE" {dog soldiers}

  (–) "TO CONQUER" {war eagles}

False-Data: 'God' has 'died of a broken heart' because we wouldn't stop fighting. So you agree to be afraid to fight.

  [Hellfire Inc. (loc) — Frankfort, Germany]

[3. GROUPS (Sphere 3)]

53. "TO ORGANIZE" {file clerk}

  (–) "TO DISORGANIZE" {super-villain}

False-Data: If everyone's postulates were 'equal', all would be chaos. So you agree that the postulates of a 'group' are senior (superior) to the postulates of any one individual.

  [Hellfire Inc. (loc) — London, England]

54. "TO COOPERATE" {*robots*}

   (–) "TO INDIVIDUATE" {*train-engine*}

False-Data: (?)

  [*Hellfire Inc. (loc)*—in orbit]

55. "TO PARTICIPATE" {*merfolk*}

   (–) "TO DEBASE" {*elephant-girl*}

      (or "TO WITHDRAW")

False-Data: We only 'think' that we are living life when really we are all living in a mass-*Implant*, and the next *'item'* is always coming at us. So you agree that you cannot do anything about it (or affect reality).

  [*Hellfire Inc. (loc)*—Capetown, S. Africa]

56. "TO EXPAND" {*mouse railroad engineer*}

   (–) "TO CONTRACT" {*maniac/psycho*}

False-Data: (?)

  [*Hellfire Inc. (loc)*—Edinburgh, Scotland]

[2. **HOME** (*Sphere 2*)]

57. "TO JOIN" {*cat people*}

   (–) "TO SEPARATE" {*black-cat*}

False-Data: We all join together in agreement to bring about reality. If any one of us really broke that agreement, then the whole thing would fall apart. So you agree that you must keep all agreements made.

[*Hellfire Inc. (loc)* —Orleans, France]

58. "TO REPRODUCE" {*insect invader*}
  (–) "TO INFEST" {*insects*}
      (or "BLANKET")

False-Data: Whenever someone 'reproduces', they are lessened by it. If this were not the case, the *Universe* would be filled up and there would be nothing left. So you agree to be 'less' whenever you reproduce (or 'divide').

[*Hellfire Inc. (loc)* —Calcutta, India]

59. "TO SATISFY" {*cavemen*}
  (–) "TO RIDICULE" {*moron*}

False-Data: Only 'God' is 'absolute'; and the *Universe* is the 'transient state'. So you agree that the *Universe*, itself, is 'unsatisfying' —and only *The Jewel* and spreading

The Jewel is satisfying.

[*Hellfire Inc. (loc)*—Peking (Beijing), China]

60. "TO CARE (FOR)" {*bird girl*}

   (–) "TO TORTURE" {*devil-pincers*}

False-Data: The only thing that will truly make people happy is to merge with 'God'. So you agree to care for others and help them to accept 'God' (and not rebel no matter how much they suffer).

[*Hellfire Inc. (loc)*—Acapulco, Mexico]

[1. SELF/BODY (*Sphere 1*)]

61. "TO EXPERIENCE" {*bear*}
      (or "TO FEEL")

   (–) "TO DEADEN" {*death-goddess*}

False-Data: (?)

[*Hellfire Inc. (loc)*—Canton, China]

62. "TO REPLENISH" {*a Sumerian*}

   (–) "TO AGE" {*father-time*}

False-Data: Everything that exists follows a cycle of 'create–survive–destroy', and things can only be replenished for so long. So you agree to age and die.

[*Hellfire Inc. (loc)*—Jerusalem]

63. "TO EAT" {*tiger*}

(–) "TO POISON" {*spider*}

False-Data: When you eat something, you gain energy from the spirit of what you've eaten. So you agree that you are infested by spirits.

[*Hellfire Inc. (loc)*—Kenya, Africa]

64. "TO ENDURE" {*pyramid*}

(–) "TO DISSIPATE" {*mummy*}

False-Data: Only 'God' persists; the *Universe* does not persist. So you agree that the only way you can 'endure' is to become 'one' with 'God'—aiding in 'his' purpose to conquer and permeate all beings.

[*Hellfire Inc. (loc)*—Egypt]

"BLACK-BOX" CONTROL-IMPLANTS
(*Experimental Research*)

The *"New Thought"* movement emerged strongly at the beginning of the *20th Century*. Then, waves of *"World War"* slowed its progress, and the spread of its information. But, in the aftermath of *WWII*, in the wake of *Roswell*, and in the shadows of *Atomic* and *Nuclear bombs*, the *"New Thought"* experienced a fierce resurgence in the early 1950s—hoping to provide a solution to a troubled planet, and a cure for the heavily *fragmented Human Condition*.

The *"Black-Box Control Implant"* was the first *spiritual implant* discovered by experimental *New Thought* practitioners. But, it was an entirely new *concept*, for which there was little reference. Anything about the subject spreading up from the underground usually became misunderstood as being part of an even more materialist-type of *"alien-implanting"* that pertained to tiny *mechanical-devices* inserted in the *physical body.*

In spite of how long *spiritual implanting* has been suspected as being a part of the *Human Condition,* the type of *systematic* approach that we might take today to handle this knowledge was simply not available at that time. The idea of *"command-lines"* or *"processing-out"* was not a part of that understanding. So, while this may be the *first Implant* discovered, surprisingly little was known about it directly until relatively recently.

This *Implant* has been used by various *"alien-forces"* for the sole purpose of *"controlling earthbound Human populations"* — while at the same time, typically setting themselves up as *"gods."* Portable devices were even given to ancient *"priests"* (those selected to propagate the *"will of the gods"* on *Earth*) to set up in the *"temp-*

les" and use on other *Humans*. And while an individual is likely to think of "historical" *Mesopotamia, Greece,* or the ancient *Far East*: the nature of this *Implant* extends further on the *Backtrack of Earth* to much earlier civilizations that have long since disappeared—like *Atlantis* and *Lemuria* and even earlier than that.

The *Implanting-gimmick* involves *energy-waves* that induce *pain* on the *items* "they" don't want you to do; *pleasure* on the *items* "they" want you to do. As opposed to other earlier *Implanting-Incidents* on the *Backtrack*, this one is more "physical" in its construction and simple in design. It was meant to be easily distributable. Though operating "cheaper portable" ones often resulted in a *"backfire"* (by design) on the individual that was doing the *Implanting*, so that they would also receive some of its effects.

Based on how it has been perceived: the *waves* are projected from a *"black-box"* on a tripod. This *"black-box"* had a "crank" on it, like a *grinder* or *sifter*, which was turned in one direction or another to generate the *wave*. In some ways, it also resembles an old-style *camera*—and the *beam* of the *wave* may be focused on one area; in this case, a specific part of the *Body*. A person operating it would appear very much like an old-time *"organ-grinder."*

During the *incident*: the following *Platform* (series of *command-items*) is projected (as *"pleasure"* or *"pain"* *energy-waves*) at each of the following areas of the *Body*:

1. *Forehead* (*third eye/pineal gland*); 2. *Left Eye*; 3. *Right Eye*; 4. *Mouth*; 5. *Left Shoulder*; 6. *Right Shoulder*; 7. *Chest*; 8. *Stomach*; 9. *Genitals*.

To *process-out* the *Implant*, a *Seeker* *"Spots"* the intense *sensation-wave* (*pain* or *pleasure*) hitting them (in an area of the *Body*) along with the *line-item*. A *Seeker* uses their *attention* to "contact" the *item/wave* impression (similar to "recall") until it no longer *registers* on a *GSR-Meter* (*biofeedback device*).

[Start with "*Forehead*" and *run* each of the following *items* on it, one at a time, making sure each one is completely *defragmented* of *turbulent charge*.]

PLEASURE-PAIN IMPLANT-PLATFORM

1.1.X {*pain*} TO BE EVERYTHING
1.2.X {*pleasure*} TO BE NOTHING

2.1.X {*pain*} TO KNOW
2.2.X {*pleasure*} TO NOT-KNOW

3.1.X {*pain*} TO BE ORIENTED
3.2.X {*pleasure*} TO BE DISORIENTED

4.1.X {*pain*} TO BE CAUSE
4.2.X {*pleasure*} TO BE EFFECT

5.1.X {*pain*} TO BE POWERFUL
5.2.X {*pleasure*} TO BE WEAK

6.1.X {*pain*} TO BE INDEPENDENT
6.2.X {*pleasure*} TO BE OBEDIENT

7.1.X *{pain}* TO PROJECT ENERGY

7.2.X *{pleasure}* TO PUT OUT NO ENERGY

8.1.X *{pain}* TO OPERATE AT A DISTANCE

8.2.X *{pleasure}* TO NOT OPERATE AT A DISTANCE

9.1.X *{pain}* TO INFLUENCE REMOTELY

9.2.X *{pleasure}* TO NOT INFLUENCE REMOTELY

10.1.X *{pain}* TO PERCEIVE AT A DISTANCE

10.2.X *{pleasure}* TO NOT PERCEIVE AT A DISTANCE

11.1.X *{pain}* TO DO THINGS WITH THE MIND

11.2.X *{pleasure}* TO DO NOTHING WITH THE MIND

12.1.X *{pain}* TO BE FREE

12.2.X *{pleasure}* TO BE RESTRAINED

13.1.X *{pain}* TO FIND OUT

13.2.X *{pleasure}* TO NEVER FIND OUT

14.1.X *{pain}* TO REVEAL THIS

14.2.X {*pleasure*} TO NEVER REVEAL THIS

15.1.X {*pain*} TO DISAGREE WITH THIS IMPLANT

15.2.X {*pleasure*} TO AGREE WITH THIS IMPLANT

16.1.X {*pain*} TO REMEMBER THIS IMPLANT

16.2.X {*pleasure*} TO FORGET THIS IMPLANT

17.1.X {*pain*} TO NEVER IMPLANT OTHERS

17.2.X {*pleasure*} TO GIVE THIS IMPLANT TO OTHERS

18.1.X {*pain*} TO NEVER BE IMPLANTED AGAIN

18.2.X {*pleasure*} TO WANT THIS IMPLANT AGAIN

INDIVIDUATION IMPLANT-PLATFORM

The following *Platform* is not a part of the former *incident*, but may likely involve some kind of "*Black-Box*" as it was located on the *Backtrack* almost simultaneously with the *"first Implant"* —but again little was known about it (*"command-lines,"* &tc.).

Although it is considered an *"alien-im-plant"* (used by technologically advanced societies in *this Universe*), it is unclear if it is used on *Earth*, or only among the more advanced *"space races"* (on *"starships,"* &tc.). Again, little is known about it, except that it is used on "prisoners-of-war" before returning them to their homes; or as a way of making prisoners an *"anti-so-cial spy"* before releasing them back to their own side.

Here, we simply have some *command-lines* that can be *defragmented*.

1. TO SEPARATE
2. TO BE AN INDIVIDUAL
3. TO BE THE ONLY ONE
4. ONLY YOU CAN BE GOD
5. ONLY YOU CAN CREATE
6. ONLY YOU CAN BE CAUSE

7. ONLY YOU CAN KNOW
8. ONLY YOU CAN WIN
9. ONLY YOU CAN CHANGE
10. ONLY YOU CAN REASON
11. ONLY YOU CAN CONSTRUCT
12. ONLY YOU CAN BE BEAUTIFUL
13. ONLY YOU CAN RULE
14. ONLY YOU CAN ENLIGHTEN
15. ONLY YOU CAN INFLUENCE
16. ONLY YOU CAN OWN (HAVE)
17. ONLY YOU CAN BE ALIVE
18. ONLY YOU CAN CONTROL
19. ONLY YOU CAN ORGANIZE
20. ONLY YOU CAN BE ADMIRED
21. ONLY YOU CAN ENDURE
22. ONLY YOU CAN BE AN INDIVIDUAL
23. YOU ARE THE ONLY ONE

RESEARCHING PENALTY-UNIVERSES
(*Advanced Technical Research*)

Understanding *"Implanted Penalty-Universes"* (IPU) is a critical component to upper-level *Systemology* and the *Ascension Path*. Our *Systemology* is currently the only *"New Thought"* tradition that works with this data. The following describes research-methods used to discover this information. The original *research-actions* tended to "stir up" as much as they *defragmented*; but this was necessary for collecting additional details.

[IPU are introduced in *AT#4*, along with *basic processing* instructions. That information will be necessary for applying this section. You will also need to refer to the list of *basic* IPU-*Goals* and *negative* IPU-*Goals* given previously in this current manual. This more recently refined procedure is appropriate for *New Standard A.T.* (*Keys to the Kingdom*) as both *defrag-processing* and a *research-action*. However, it is entirely dependent on having access to that existing data collected for IPU (and all other course lessons and manuals).]

Total Defragmentation of the IPU is too steep of a gradient for any *Seeker* to approach all at once. The original intention for focusing research-efforts on IPU emerged only after realizing how much of their *systematic structure* and *symbolism* kept reemerging in *later* (more recent) *Implants* and *incidents*. Then, as more *archetypes* and significant "themes" continued to resurface, it became a research-area of increasing interest. It is also an incredibly *advanced* area to fully handle and investigate.

There are two *classes* (or *groups*) of *processes* applied in this *procedure*. "Class-2" requires having *run* all of "Class-1." You will be handling the basic *64* IPU-*Goals*, and their *64* "*inversions*"—the *negative-goals* listed in the previous section titled: "*The False Jewel of Knowledge.*" You will also need to use IPU-*Platforms #1* and *#2* provided in *AT#4*.

You start by lightly *processing* the basic

Goals (similar to what is described in *AT#4*). As you start *running* deeper into the IPU-content, more of *"What Is"* becomes accessible. Then you start adding *Class-1 processing-actions* gradually until you are *running* all of the steps on each of the basic *Goals*. After you are getting comfortable handling basic *Goals*, you can start to treat the *negative Goals* using a different method (the *"Treadmill Platform"* given later in this manual). [For *Class-2*, see the later section *"Actual Goals & Basic Purposes"* (and steps of the *Standard Procedure for IPU* given in *AT#4*).]

Similar to what is experienced with other *Implant-Platforms*: initially encountering hundreds of *items* can be slow-going. When you first approach a new *pattern*, you'll find that you have to be much more diligent and meticulous in *processing-out* each individual *item*. Eventually, you can *defragment* whole groups of *items*, just by *"Spotting"* the first one in a set. Then it starts to get much faster; where you *contact* the very first *item* of a *pattern*, *Spot* various *Goals*, and completely *disperse* an IPU-*terminal* from your *reality-machinery* with only a minute or two of *processing-time*.

Processing-time at *Systemology Level-8* usually consists of approximately equal amounts of: handling *entities*; increasing *spiritual ability* (with *Wizard Level* exercises); and, *research-actions*. This might not always apply to one single *session*; but an *upper-level Seeker* should make sure that they are balancing actual *personal development* with other work. *Defragmenting* IPU *terminals/symbolism* "frees up" a lot of entangled *energetic-mass*. To avoid feeling a *"loss of having something,"* it is important to exercise certainty on *"creative abilities."*

A *Seeker* typically selects which *Goal* (IPU) to *run* based on an *assessment* of the *16 Dynamic Systems*. One of the *Dynamic Systems* will *register* strongest; then you *assess* from the *4 Goals* listed under that *system*. The exact sequence that an individual experienced various original IPU is not likely the same as someone else. However, *later* (more recent) *Implants* did *restimulate* them in specific sequences. The common ones are:

- The natural sequence of the *Dynamic Systems*: from *16* to *1* (*Create* down to *Endure*)—or the reverse: from *1* to *16*. If the inversions are involved, the *negative Goals* are *alternated* with the *positive Goals* (such as with the *incident* that originally established the *negative-items*).

- The natural sequence, like above; but all *64* basic *Goals* come first (*Create* down to *Endure*), *followed by* the *64 negative Goals* in their reverse dynamic order—*Dissipate* (for *Dynamic System 1*) to *Destroy* (*System 16*).

- The *Dynamic Systems* sequence occur in pairs: the upper *Arc* collapsing into the corresponding lower *Sphere*. These are:

16 and *8*; *15* and *7*; *14* and *6*; *13* and *5*;
12 and *4*; *11* and *3*; *10* and *2*; then *9* and
1. Or, the same pattern may occur in an
ascending sequence (from *1* to *16*). And
again, if inversions are involved, they
might either *alternate* with the basic
Goals, or *follow* after them (in a reverse
sequence).

CLASS–1 IPU PROCEDURE

A. IPU-PLATFORM #1. [*AT#4*] The starting point of all IPU procedures. Once the
IPU is contacted, *all items* should either be
registering as *charged*, or they should be
completely clear from previous processing. If a particular *item* doesn't give a
Meter-read: pause and *imagine/create* ex-
actly what the *item* means, then try to
Spot the actual *item* in the incident again.
If unresolved: continue with some of the
steps below and return to this one.

B. Check for any *Harmful-Acts* and/or
hold-backs/hold-outs (*&tc.*) connected with

"doing" this *Goal*. *Spot* these and any associated *justifications*.

C. "*Spot the Hellfire Incident Location*" (on *Earth*); notice the false manifestation of the IPU that was placed there during the *incident*. The *incident*, itself, is introduced in *AT#5*; but the locations needed here are listed previously in *this* manual (along with the *negative-goals*) in the section titled "*The False Jewel of Knowledge.*"

D. "*Spot the Pyramid Location*" (from a mass-*Implant* taking place on *Earth* in a prior *Universe*); and *Spot* the "face" of the *Goal-terminal* (a "beingness" that represents the *Goal*) within the *Pyramid*. [*AT#4*]

E. "*Spot the {Goal-terminal} Saying {the 'Price' of the Goal}.*" [*AT#4*] For the *negative Goals*: spot the *inverted Terminal* saying, "*This means an end to..*"

F. "*Spot Places Where {Goal-terminal} Is Not.*" Then: "*Spot Places In The Penalty-Universe Where You Are Not.*"

G. IPU-PLATFORM #2. [AT#4] *Spot* IPU-*Symbol items*. There are a few listed in the *AT#4-directory*. Others can be *Spotted* and *defragged-by-realization*. This *Platform* is only used on basic (*positive*) *Goals*.

H. *Scan* researched IPU *details*. [AT#4]

I. Handle any current *Backtrack* restimulation. *Spot* "*What Is*," and *defrag-by-realization*.

J. Check for any *Programmed Machine-Entities* (PME) that are currently *being machinery* related to the *Goal*. [AT#5] Note that a *Seeker* should have already *defragged* the more troublesome *machinery*, and should be able to handle this step using the "*Short Version*" of PME-procedure, having each: *spot being made into a machine; spot the first time; spot making others into a machine; spot the top of IPU-Platform #1; identification cleanup (who are you?)*.

K. *Run* a "*creativeness*" *repair-action* of *ma-*

chinery related to the *Goal*. This means starting with *creating/imagining* "broken" or "decrepit" versions of the *machinery* and working your way up to "fine-quality" *machinery*; throwing some *copies* away, pushing some in from the outside, *&tc.*

L. *"Spot Something You Must Not {Goal}."* Repeat to a *release-point* for that area.

M. *"Spot People, Groups (&tc.) That You Would Permit To {Goal}."* Repeat to a *release-point* (total willingness to have others doing this *Goal*).

N. *"Spot Places Where {Goal-terminal} Would Be Safe."* Repeat to a *release-point* (total willingness to have it anywhere, or not have it anywhere, by choice).

O. *"Spot Things That The {Goal-terminal} Does Not Own."*

P. *Create/Imagine* battered and beaten versions of the *Goal-terminal* in various places, and say: *"Oh, the poor thing; see how it needs me?"*

Q. *Spot* the top of the *Failure-Implant.* They would tell you to do the *Goal* to some object and then prove how you failed. The *command-item* is: "You failed to *{Goal}*; so you must depend on others to *{Goal}* for you."

R. *Spot* any *"between-lives scene"* for the *Goal* (if known). [This may not be determined accurately until more of the *fragmentation* is *dispersed*.]

S. *Realization*: the collapse of the basic *Goal* becomes the perceived *justification* for (doing) the *negative Goal*.

T. *"Spot The {Goal-terminal} Saying, 'Do You Want To Achieve The Power {To Goal}'."* This occurs during a *"between-lives sequence."* There is a false promise made to you about the *Goal* that pulls you deeper into it.

U. *"Spot The Desire To Shift To The Negative-Goal, So As To Be Rid Of This Penalty-*

Universe."

V. *Run* "*creativeness*" (*imagining copies*: throwing away; pushing in, *&tc.*) on any objects or interesting things used in the IPU. [*Running* "*creativeness*" at *Wizard-Levels* increases *certainty* on the *ability-to-have* without *compulsively creating* or remaining attached to anything *unknowingly*.]

W. Check for any other *entities* "stirred-up" (or awakened) by this procedure.

X. *Spot* the first few lines of IPU-PLATFORM #1 again.

BETWEEN-LIVES "JUST-CONS"

There are "*Justification Considerations*" that are *Implanted* during *between-lives periods*. This is likely to have occurred earlier on the *Backtrack*. The *definitions* and *symbols* come from the first *Agreements-Universe*, though there is some relationship to the IPU. This *Implant* leads to *considering* "undesirable things" in order to make IPU-*terminals* (others) wrong.

[This advanced research may apply to *"between-lives scenery"* for IPU-handling (above). Note that there may be minor errors on this list. More research-testing is still needed.]

The top of the *Platform* is:

TO BE RIGHT IS NATIVE STATE.

The following *items* will easily *defrag-on-realization.*

1. The agreeing dog says: *"They're wrong because they disagree with everything."*
2. The good bear says: *"They're wrong because they're nasty."*
3. The causative salesman says: *"They're wrong because they chose to be affected."*
4. The free horse says: *"They're wrong because they let themselves be enslaved."*
5. The beautiful cherub says: *"They're wrong because they're ugly."*

6. The logical alligator says: *"They're wrong because they're illogical."*

7. The winning seagull says: *"They're wrong because they're losers."*

8. The healthy flamingo says: *"They're wrong because they're sick."*

9. The enduring dinosaur says: *"They're wrong because they lack persistence."*

10. The skillful bee says: *"They're wrong because they're incompetent."*

11. The interested fish says: *"They're wrong because they have no interest in anything."*

12. The moving rock says: *"They're wrong because they wouldn't move."*

13. The certain computer says: *"They're wrong because they're always confused."*

14. The pleasurable ostrich says: *"They're wrong because they hurt people."*

15. The cube who is right says *"They're wrong because they were made to be wrong to begin with."*

16. The giant who sees truly says: *"They're wrong because they imagine*

everything."

17. The visible statue says: *"They're wrong because they keep everything hidden."*

18. The present jellyfish says: *"They're wrong because they're never there when they should be."*

19. The smart ibis-bird says: *"They're wrong because they're stupid."*

20. The just flame says: *"They're wrong because they're unjust."*

21. The stork who brings order says: *"They're wrong because they make everything chaotic."*

22. The wakeful whale says: *"They're wrong because they're always asleep."*

23. The humorous seal says: *"They're wrong because they're too serious."*

24. The squirrel who plans says: *"They're wrong because they leave everything to chance."*

25. The mechanical man who is whole says: *"They're wrong because they keep falling apart and fragmenting."*

26. The strong robot says: *"They're wrong because they're weak."*

27. The real peacock says: *"They're wrong because they're unreal."*

28. The independent monkey says: *"They're wrong because they let themselves be owned."*

29. The infinite spirit says: *"They're wrong because they're located."*

30. The courageous lion says: *"They're wrong because they're cowards."*

31. The knowing owl says: *"They're wrong because they don't know anything."*

32. The sharing raccoon says: *"They're wrong because they're greedy."*

33. The calm deer says: *"They're wrong because they're nervous."*

34. The sea urchin who is different says: *"They're wrong because they're all the same."*

35. The outgoing turtle says: *"They're wrong because they're withdrawn."*

36. The oriented wooden man says:

"They're wrong because they're disoriented."

37. The silent cat says: *"They're wrong because they're noisy."*
38. The started snail says: *"They're wrong because they let themselves be stopped."*
39. The ethical octopus says: *"They're wrong because they're all criminals."*
40. The reasonable knight says: *"They're wrong because they're arbitrary and have no reason for what they do."*
41. The responsible possum says: *"They're wrong because they're irresponsible."*
42. The independent corn-man says: *"They're wrong because they follow the crowd and wouldn't act independently."*
43. The helpful caterpillar says: *"They're wrong because they harm everything."*
44. The alive raggedy doll says: *"They're wrong because they're dead."*
45. The timeless mountain says: *"They're wrong because they cannot endure."*

46. The social potato man says: *"They're wrong because they're all anti-social."*
47. The trusting rabbit says: *"They're wrong because they distrust everything."*
48. The remembering elephant says: *"They're wrong because they forget everything."*
49. The young gorilla says: *"They're wrong because they're old."*
50. The perceptive mouse says: *"They're wrong because they're blind."*
51. The loving flower says: *"They're wrong because they hate."*
52. The serene swan says: *"They're wrong because they're always getting upset."*
53. The big ant says: *"They're wrong because they're small."*
54. The fast horse girl says: *"They're wrong because they're slow."*
55. The industrious donkey says: *"They're wrong because they're lazy."*
56. The truthful walrus says: *"They're wrong because they lie."*
57. The pleasant eagle says: *"They're*

wrong because they act horribly."

58. The harmonious angel says: *"They're wrong because they create discord."*
59. The participating kangaroo says: *"They're wrong because they wouldn't participate."*
60. The wise alligator person says: *"They're wrong because they're all fools."*
61. The unicorn who has faith says: *"They're wrong because they're distrustful."*
62. The good snake says: *"They're wrong because they're all evil."*
63. The feeling porcupine says: *"They're wrong because they have no feeling."*
64. The creative fool says: *"They're wrong because they're destructive."*

THE "AGREEMENTS UNIVERSE"
(*Advanced Technical Research*)

The *"Agreements-Universe Implant"* is that *entry-point incident* through which we arrived at the *Agreements Universe* (see *AT#1*)—which began as a simple *agreed-upon Space* in which to *Create* "things" and "play" *Games*. The original *Jewel of Knowledge* impressed upon us the need to enforce a common set of *shared-agreements* in order to operate within the same frame-of-reference or *Universe*.

This *Implant* is unique in that we all went through it by choice, rather than being forced. We "solved" an era of individualized misaligned *Spaces* by constructing an *Implant* that installed a common set of definitions and *reality-agreements*. We rushed to throw ourselves into it and came out into the first *agreed-upon Space*.

As described in *AT#1*: *Alpha-Spirits* divided up into teams, with each working on one "sub-universe" of the *Implant*. Then they were all combined together, and the result became the *Agreements-Universe*. But, of course, each individual was only really aware of the one part that they contributed to working on. The full "set" was not known to anyone until we experienced the *incident*.

Creating components of *reality* without knowing the others meant some things didn't line up or correspond properly to one another—and this obviously led to some problems. It is probably the most *basic* of all the trouble we have since gotten into.

But, notice here that this was not *enforced* on an *Alpha-Spirit*, it was done by choice; and an individual is not likely to fully "drop" these *agreements* (even during *processing*) unless they are completely willing to "drop" contact and communication

117

with *everyone else* that also went into this trap.

Therefore, the best we can hope from the current research is to *defrag* some of the *turbulence* from the *incident* and increase *Awareness* on the wide-view of the exact nature of the *Game* that is actually going on.

We can't use *processing* to pull out of the *Universe-Laws* and *agreements* all at once —since such would simply result in chaos anyways—but we can follow a gradient *Pathway* of increasing *freedom* and lessening *barriers*.

Eventually, we might reach a point where we can all get together and go back to change the basic-level *reality-agreements* around a bit so that we can have a better game. But, in the meantime, we also have the IPU to *process-out*, and those really act as a *basic* foundation to our *fragmentation* —since they *were enforced*. But, that does-not mean we cannot gain benefit now from delving further on the *Backtrack* to see the *agreements*.

The *Agreements-Universe Implant* (AUI) isn't full of hidden implications and subtle meanings. It simply puts up quite a "stack" of simpleminded conceptual definitions, such as you would display for children's educational programs. As such, the definitions are not in *"words"* or *"commands."*

The definitions present dividing lines that separate a concept into two classes — or else a dichotomy of opposites, such as *"Good"* and *"Bad."* But, if you are imagining a clean "line" running down a sheet of paper dividing these things, you'd be wrong. The definitions on one "sheet" do not necessarily align with those in the remainder of the "stack." For example, there is another appearance of *"Good"* on the agreements-list that means *"Holy"* as opposed to the one above that means *"Nice."*

The incident begins with being a part of a crowd and "rushing to get into agreement." Then you pass through an *inverted golden-triangle*, which is the symbol of the *Agreements-Universe*: representing all things focusing down to a single point of *agreement*. Then you get the first *"item-line"* of the *Platform*.

The AUI-*Platform* starts identical to the first several *item-lines* of IPU-*Platform #1* (see *AT#4*); but instead of a *"goal,"* the word "AGREE" is inserted. The top of the *Platform* (1.1.1) is then:

TO AGREE IS NATIVE STATE.

The basic sequence of the AUI is:

1. An introduction. Like IPU-*Platform #1.*

2. A series of definition sub-universes.

3. A period where you make various *agreements* (after being shown the need for each, you *agree* to it).

The top of the AUI can be *run* this way:

A. *"Spot 'rushing to get into agreement'."*

B. *"Spot 'going through the inverted golden-triangle'."*

C. *"Spot:* TO AGREE IS NATIVE STATE."

D. *"Look prior to this; Spot 'deciding that you need to agree'."*

E. (If necessary) *"Spot 'getting others to decide to agree'."*

F. (If necessary) *"Spot 'working on building the Agreements-Universe'."*

The *Platform* then runs just like IPU-*Platform #1*, down through *line-item-*`1.6.3`:

TO AGREE IS THE BASIS FOR ALL DECISIONS.

The next six *line-items* are:

TO AGREE IS TO ACHIEVE ___.

And the keywords are: *Knowledge, Power, Wisdom, Affinity (or Likingness), Reality,* and *Communication.*

121

The next *item*:

TO AGREE IS TO PLAY THE GAME.

Then all *64* of the IPU-*Goals* are each given in the form of:

TO AGREE IS TO {*Goal*}.

Note: this may actually be the first origination of the IPU-*Goals* and the *Dynamic Systems*.

Then: TO AGREE IS TO KNOW THE
MEANING OF THINGS.

And then the definitions come. For each one you enter a kind of cathedral-looking building through an archway (or maybe it's another *inverted triangle*). The first *item-lines* of each is:

TO AGREE IS TO KNOW THE MEANING
OF ___.

The dichotomy would be inserted for the *item* — such as *"goodness and badness"* — followed by a pair of scenes (one to represent each side of the definition) for each of the *16 Dynamic Systems*. These "scenes" have not yet really been researched. One of the early ones shows a *"Good Bear"* building things and then a *"Bad Bear"* comes and kicks them down. Basic, simple, imagery of this nature. One of the challenges is that later (more recent) *incidents* have added more layers of *fragmentation* over these definitions and *agreements*, which requires clearing out before we can see more.

The following AUI-*list* was compiled by *assessment* rather than our researchers *running* each one. This is still a tentative sequence; but since it does *run* well, it's become as close to a standard as we currently have. [It is possible that it should also include *"Serene/Upset"* somewhere in it.]

1. Agreeing / Disagreeing
2. Good (Nice) / Bad {*bears*}
3. Causative / Effected
4. Winning / Losing {*seagull*}
5. Logical / Illogical {*alligator*}

6. Beautiful / Ugly

7. Strong / Weak

8. Interested / Disinterested

9. Certain / Confused

10. Healthy / Sick

11. Sane / Crazy (Truth / Hallucination)

12. Free / Enslaved

13. Enduring / Transient

14. Fast / Slow

15. Right / Wrong

16. Present / Absent (Always / Never)

17. Moving / Stopped (Motion / No-Motion)
        (Changing / Fixed)

18. Seen / Invisible

19. Gives Pleasure / Gives Pain

20. Humorous / Sullen

21. Smart / Dumb {*birds*}

22. Brings Order / Brings Chaos

23. Awake / Unconscious (Asleep) {*dogs*}

24. Just / Unjust

25. Divided / Combined

26. Real / Unreal

27. Courageous / Cowardly {*lion*}

28. Located / Infinite

29. Knowing / Ignorant

30. Owned / Available
31. Volitional / Controlled
32. Older / Younger
33. Wise / Foolish
34. Same / Different
35. Rigid / Fluid
36. Oriented / Disoriented
37. Connected / Withdrawn
38. Truthful / Deceitful
39. Ethical / Criminal
40. Skillful / Incompetent
41. Started / Stopped
42. Responsible / Irresponsible
43. Happy / Sad
44. Singularly Owned / Shared
45. Helpful / Harmful
46. Playful / Serious
47. Trusting / Distrusting
48. Alive / Dead {*raggedy doll*}
49. Loving / Hating {*flowers*}
50. Perceptive / Blind {*mice*}
51. Flexible / Fixed
52. Social / Anti-Social
53. Aware / Unaware
54. Big / Small

55. Reasonable / Arbitrary

56. Industrious / Lazy

57. Quiet / Noisy

58. Numb / Feeling

59. Harmony / Discord

60. Participating / Separated Out

61. Greedy / Sharing

62. Faith / Disbelief

63. Good (Holy) / Evil

64. Remembering / Forgetful

65. Created / Destroyed

ACTUAL GOALS & BASIC PURPOSES
(*Advanced Technical Research*)

One *Implant* that really *fragmented* our *goals* and *purposes* early on the *Backtrack*, is referred to simply as *"The Treadmill."* It was constructed in the original *"Games Universe."* It is unclear whether it was only used as general punishment *there,* or whether it was also part of the *sentencing-incident* where an individual is sent down to the *"next lower"* Universe.

A simplified version of each IPU and its *Goals* were used for this *Implant*. A sub-universe dramatizing a related *negative-Goal* was attached to the end of each one. The IPU-version establishes the *negative-Goal* by collapsing the basic (*positive*) *Goal* down to *zero*—to a point of complete apathy, overwhelm, and solidity. Then it is dramatized to essentially "*un-manifest*" everything until you "go out the bottom" of the *Alpha-Awareness* scale.

At the end, you've basically destroyed everything so that there is no "*universe*" left. This leaves you with a false "*native state*" (which is a consideration of one's *basic original nature*) that is made to equal the "*native state*" at the top of the *next* basic (*positive*) *Goal.* This ongoing "scrolling quality" of the *Implant* is the only reason we call it "*The Treadmill.*"

One can almost liken this to an old-time cartoon, where the individual remains mostly stationary, while the background scenery "scrolls" to give an illusion of movement and travel. The bottom of the final *negative-Goal* was connected to the top of the first basic (*positive*) *Goal* again, which just kept one moving through all *128* total *Goals*. Once the *Implanting* really starts to take hold, the *Alpha-Spirit* gets a "spinning" sensation.

The basic *Platform* for "*The Treadmill*" begins just like the original IPU (*Platform #1*). [See *AT#4*] However the "*Symbols*" part (*Platform #2, &tc.*) is not used. Instead, the *Implant* goes straight to this *item*:

TO {*goal*} IS TO POSTULATE BEING THE {*terminal*}.

Then a handful of *items* duplicating the IPU scenery occur. But the basic (*positive*) *Goals* end differently. Once the *terminal's body* dies, you are able to "*exteriorize*" from the grave. Once you are floating above the grave, then the *items* from the "*Treadmill Crossover Platform*" begin. This has you abandon the basic *Goal*, then shifts you into *negative-Goal*.

The *fourth item* of the *Crossover Platform* [STEP-D of the sequence (below)] is the end of the basic (*positive*) *Goal*. When *running* it, you should spot the top of the basic *Goal* ("*native state*" item) at this point, because some B.E. and *Fused-Groups* (*AT#5*) are stuck holding on this point, trying to avoid the start of the *negative-Goal*. Use the above information and the IPU details given in *AT#4* for *running* basic *Goals*. The following *Crossover Platform* is *only* used for *negative-Goals* in this *incident*.

TREADMILL CROSSOVER PLATFORM

The *Crossover Platform* begins at the point of the *incident* when you are floating about the grave of the dead IPU-*terminal*. This *Platform* is used for the *negative-Goals* as they appear in "*The Treadmill*"; but this is also the experimental procedure used for handling specifically *negative* IPU-*Goals* wherever they appear in an *Implant* (such as the original *"False Jewel"* given earlier in this manual). This is the sequence:

A. TO {*positive goal*} IS TO REGRET EVER HAVING {*positive goal-ed*}.

B. TO {*positive goal*} IS TO ABANDON THE GOAL OF {*positive goal*}.

C. TO ABANDON {*positive goal*} IS TO SURVIVE.

D. TO ABANDON {*positive goal*} IS TO FORGET EVER HAVING {*positive goal-ed*}.

   (*"Spot the 'native state' item at the top of Platform #1."*)

E. {You begin to hate.}

F. {You decide to get even.}

G. {You choose a new goal.}

H. {You choose to (*negative goal*).}

I. IN THE BEGINNING, NOW, AND FOREVER, IS THE DECISION; AND

THE DECISION IS TO {*negative goal*}.

J. TO {*negative goal*} IS THE ULTIMATE PURPOSE.

K. TO {*negative goal*} IS TO ACHIEVE ___.
   (The *keywords/items* are: *Freedom, Success, Enlightenment, Truth, Beauty, Knowledge, Power, Control, Respect, &tc.* Usually you only have to lightly spot a few of these to contact the next *item* below.)

L. TO {*negative goal*} IS TO BE THE {*negative terminal*}.
   (At this point of the incident, the *negative-Goal terminal* appears.)

When *processing-out negative-Goals*:
   Spot the following data (*where available*).

1. The "*inversion scene*" (used in later *Implants*).
2. This *Implant* making you abandon the basic (*positive*) *Goal*.
3. The top of the basic *Goal* ("*native state*" item).

131

4. The action of the *negative-terminal* in doing *Goal*.
5. The *Hellfire Incident* location.
6. The *Pyramid* location.
7. "*This Means An End To* ___" statement said by the *negative-terminal*.
8. The "*Survive*" statement said by the *negative-terminal*.

OPPOSITIONAL FRAGMENTATION

Games, *Goals*, and *Purposes*, are critical components of our *Systemology*, because they are key to fully understanding the thoughts and behaviors inherent in the *Human Condition*. This is an area that is often more challenging to *confront*, because an individual is likely keeping "one eye" on any signs, or validation, of whatever their own *Goals* and *Purposes* were before they were all *fragmented*. Of course, such is not really within view until the layers of *fragmentation* have been stripped off of whatever we were once interested in.

Developing experimental material for researching the original *"Oppositional-
Goals-Problem Implant"* was among the
more difficult research-efforts (perhaps
second only to the *"Big Splitter Incident"*
that is covered in the next section). One
of the reasons is that early on, while some
gains were made, these areas often
stirred-up a lot of trouble for researchers.
[Review relevant data in *AT#1* and *AT#2*
before handling this section.]

This *Implanting-Incident* occurs while going down a long *"ringed-tube"* as a
transfer-shift between the *"Thought-Energy
Universe"* and what became the *"Conflict
Universe."* Each of the *"rings"* installs another *"oppositional-goal-problem"* as you
pass it. It is structured after the IPU-*Goals*.
[After this transition, an *Alpha-Spirit*
ceases to maintain a *Beingness* as an *en-
ergy-sphere-type "body"* and starts to
Identify with a more material structure.]

This *Implant* installs each *Goal* with *imp-*

rints of 5 different *Identity-phases*. They are:

1. *Goal-terminal*
2. *Oppositional-terminal* (who becomes the "target" of *harmful-acts*)
3. *Encouraging-terminal* (who wants *Goal*, enforces *Goal*; acts as a third party)
4. *Discouraging-terminal* (who doesn't want *Goal*, inhibits *Goal*; you are constantly *justifying* the *Goal* and your *harmful-acts* to this person, which makes the *considerations* "stick")
5. *A Victim* (who unjustly suffers from your *harmful-acts*; this *imprints* you with *regret*)

The experience of each *Goal* is only a short *Platform* of "*This Means __*" *symbols*, which explain the 5 different *Identity-phases* (or "*personas*") and what's *supposed* to be *expected* from the "scenery." Then the *Implant-Platform* installs a few "*splitter-items*" while an energy-wave is emitted to *enforce* a 5-way split.

At this point, your *Awareness/Beingness* "splits" into *5 fragments*, so that *you* actually become *all 5 phases*, but compartmented (hidden) from yourself. Now you are all ready for the "scenery" to begin—but it doesn't; instead you find yourself at the next "ring" of the "tube" and getting the next *Goal* in the sequence. Each time, you are expecting some *pocket-universe drama* to unfold; but you just end up at the next "ring."

After the *Implanting-Incident* ends with the final *Goal*, you end up in the *Conflict-Universe*. There is no "imaginary scenery" or "pocket-universe" where you play things out. All of that *fragmented charge* that is accumulated from experiencing all *64 Goals* (multiplied by *splitting* into *5 phases* for each) of the *Implant* is brought down to the *Conflict-Universe* and dramatized there—in an *actual Shared-Universe*. It is *you* that ends up enacting all the actual events in "real life"—but by following the *implanted* "pattern-of-action."

Your primary activity in the *Conflict-Universe* was running around unbeknownst to 5 *split-Identities*, and then trying to *align* with the other four connected to the same *Goal*. You try to be the basic *Goal-terminal*, but your *viewpoint* is really from any of the 5, depending on the circumstances. *Systematically*: while this is occurring, you have a *sub-identity* attached to (or "in") each of the other 4 *phases*; and you, in turn, also are infected by a *sub-identity* of each of the others. This holds you in a specific *phase* and contributes to events.

Early on, in the *Conflict-Universe*, this activity all played out with great precision. Later, it became quite convoluted, and none of the activities or *phases* properly aligned with each other. Yet, we still had 5 *hidden viewpoints* (*per Goal*) running around and causing trouble in attempts to keep the *implanted-drama* going.

The fact remains that we really *are creating* our own *opposition*, even if *unknowingly*; and most of our *Awareness* or *spiritual power* (or ZU) is still entangled in doing this in present-time. Things are so out-of-alignment in *this Physical Universe*, and in such a way that, with hundreds of these *split-fragments* all working at cross-purposes, the end result is a balance of forces that keeps things fairly "solid" and difficult to change purely by *Alpha-Thought* (*postulate*).

When *running* the *Imprinting-Incident*, the "This Means ___" items are accompanied by 3-D *images* (*Imprints*) similar to the IPU-*symbols* (except with different content). But this *restimulates* the "top" of the IPU—whereas most *Implants* stir-up the "bottom." The result is a *being* that is a *super-charged maniac* ready to enthusiastically dive full into the *Goal*.

It is best to work from an established *Platform* when actually *processing-out Imp-*

lant-fragmentation (such as what a *Seeker* has been using for their *upper-level* work). However, having this data requires re-searching it. This area is not included in former manuals because it is still in a *"research-phase."* To *run* it fully would require researching specific data on each one of the *imprint-picture items* for all *64 Goals*. And "skipping" the *Imprints* for a *Goal* seems to have a tendency to turn on "depressive fatigue" until they *are* found and *run*.

Basic research to establish an experiment-al procedure (*Platform*) for *oppositional-goals-problems* (OGP) handling occurred in two stages and hit many obstacles. These were easily overcome once we started applying the *"Locational Procedure"* (*"Point To The Being You Divided From"*) after each of *item-lines 10* through *14*. This was not available for handling the *"splitting items"* when research first began. It is not indicated in the Platform, but it really is the key to using this for *defragmentation*. The *first item* is the actual *oppositional-goals-problem* (OGP) stated as a personal *consideration*. [Most, if not all, *fragmentation* will usually *disperse* by *item-line 15*.]

1. TO {goal} {target} AND {desired effect on others} OR I WILL {harmful-act}
2. THIS MEANS (to do goal)
3. THIS MEANS (desired effect)
4. THIS MEANS (harmful-act) {picture imprints it being done to the *oppositional-terminal*}
5. THIS MEANS ENCOURAGEMENT {picture imprints *encouraging-terminal*}
6. THIS MEANS DISCOURAGEMENT {picture imprints *discouraging-terminal*}
7. THIS MEANS OPPOSITION {imprint of *oppositional-terminal*}
8. THIS MEANS REGRET {picture imprints you doing the harmful-act to the *victim*}
9. THIS MEANS YOU {imprint of *basic Goal-terminal*}
10. TO {goal} IS TO BE THE {discouraging-terminal} AND DISCOURAGE

MYSELF FROM {harmful-act} AND
NEVER LET MYSELF KNOW THAT I
AM DOING THIS.

11. TO {goal} IS TO BE THE {encouraging-terminal} AND ENCOURAGE MYSELF
TO {harmful-act} AND NEVER LET
MYSELF KNOW THAT I AM DOING
THIS.

12. TO {goal} IS TO BE THE {oppositional-terminal} AND OPPOSE MYSELF
FROM {goal-ing} AND NEVER LET
MYSELF KNOW THAT I AM DOING
THIS.

13. TO {goal} IS TO BE THE {victim} AND
SUFFER UNJUSTLY AND NEVER
LET MYSELF KNOW THAT I AM
DOING THIS.

14. TO {goal} IS TO BE THE {basic-terminal} AND {do goal} AND NEVER
LET MYSELF KNOW THAT I AM
DOING THIS.

The next *command-lines* are *Implanted* simultaneously in *5 locations*; one for each *split-identity phase.* Rather than going immediately to *item-15,* better *defrag*-results have been achieved by taking each *phase* in turn and *spotting* the other 4 *phases* from that viewpoint. For example: conceiving yourself as being the *basic-terminal*, and *spotting* each of the other *phases*; then taking up being the *oppositional-terminal*, and *spotting* each of the other *phases*, &tc.

[A "cloud" of B.E. might suddenly be perceived as active during one of these "*spottings*." If so, hold the *viewpoint* for the *phase* you're on, and start *dispersing* the *entities* by *acknowledgment*, &tc. You can even run through the above mentioned *spotting-steps* a second time if you find a lot of this happening.]

After using all *5 viewpoints* to *spot* each other (as described above), you should be able to *spot item-15* in all *5 locations* simultaneously; and if so, this is usually enough to *defragment* the remaining *Implant-Platform*. At whatever point in the *Platform* that the whole "*oppositional-goals-problem*" (OGP) *disperses*, skip to the end. Note that the *5 locations* are likened to "blades" of a *5-bladed fan* that are propelling around a center *location* that your *Awareness* can't occupy.

15. TO {*Goal*} IS TO BE ALL THESE 5 OTHERS AND HIDE FROM MYSELF FOREVER

16. TO {*Goal*} IS TO BE ALL THESE 5 OTHERS AND INSPIRE MYSELF FOREVER

17. TO {*Goal*} IS TO BE ALL THESE 5 OTHERS AND COMPEL MYSELF TO RE-ENACT THIS FOREVER

18. TO {*Goal*} IS TO BE ALL THESE 5 OTHERS AND GO AROUND UNKNOWN TO MYSELF

18x. TO {*Goal*} IS TO BE ALL THESE 5 OTHERS AND COMPEL OTHERS TO RE-ENACT THIS WITH ME

[You are hit by an *energetic-mass* containing the emotion of distrust along with the *next item*.]

19. TO {*Goal*} IS TO BE ALL THESE 5 OTHERS AND AS EACH ONE, DETEST BEING ALL THE OTHERS

20. TO {*Goal*} IS TO BE ALL THESE 5 OTHERS AND AS EACH ONE, KNOW

THAT MY VIEWPOINT IS THE BEST
(compared to the others)

21. TO {*Goal*} IS TO BE ALL THESE 5
OTHERS AND DENY
RESPONSIBILITY FOR DOING THIS,
FOREVER

22. TO {*Goal*} IS TO BE SPLIT INTO 5
PARTS AND NEVER LET MYSELF
KNOW WHAT I AM DOING

   [You are impacted by a *"splitter"*
energy-beam. (Spot the impact.)]

23. TO {*Goal*} IS TO BE DIVIDED 5 WAYS
AGAINST MYSELF AND HIDE MY
ACTIONS FROM MYSELF AS I
MANIFEST ALL OF THIS

24. TO {*Goal*} IS TO BE DIVIDED 5 WAYS
AGAINST MYSELF AND NEVER
REALLY KNOW WHAT IS
HAPPENING

   [An *energy-implosion* occurs at each
of the 5 locations; each collapses and
disappears from view, leaving a *hollow-
spot* (*vacuum-of-space*).]

25. TO {*Goal*} IS TO FORGET THAT THIS
EVER HAPPENED

After *running* this procedure on a single

Goal: "*Scan*" the *Backtrack* for times when you dramatized this *Implant*; *Spot* any *harmful-acts* against others, and *spot* being in the other *viewpoints* and contributing to the activity/event-sequence. Check for any dramatization of the *Implant* in *this lifetime*; *identify* which *phase* you were in, and perform this *spotting* action on it as well.

"OGP" DATA & TERMINALS-LIST

The OGP are related to the *64* IPU-*Goals*. In addition to the *imprint-pictures* and *terminals* (*phases*), there is a unique OGP-*consideration* (*item-1*) for each *Goal*. There is limited data for this; it requires more research. But, where available, the OGP-*consideration* and associated *Identity-phases* for some *Goals* are listed below. The list is numbered based on IPU *Goal-sequencing*. The *phases* are in the *1-to-5* ordering given earlier.

1. CREATE OGP: "To create chaos and

overwhelm others or I will blow them up."

—Phases: *God, Satan/Devil, Priest, Virgin, Seer.*

3. MANIFEST OGP: "To manifest intricate ornaments and have them praised or I will cut out their guts."

—Phases: *Artisan (craftsman), Scientist, Fishmonger, Policeman, Priest.*

4. IMAGINE OGP: "To imagine fine stories and have them appreciated or I will strangle everyone."

—Phases: *Writer, Cynical Father, Actor, Critic, Publisher.*

6. UNDERSTAND OGP: "To understand secrets and make others tell (obey?) (recognize my power?) or I will stab them all."

—Phases: *Detective, Criminal, Police Captain, Businessman, Prostitute.*

8. LEARN OGP: "To learn the nature of the *Universe* and be supported or I will overwhelm them all."

—Phases: *Scientist, Preacher, Teacher, Wife, Stupid Person.*

11. COMPETE OGP: "To compete (at boxing) and have the people cheer or I will beat them all up."

—Phases: *Boxer, Newspaperman, Manager, Lover, Businessman.*

15. CHANGE OGP: "To change peoples' nature and have them all be happy about this or I will strike them all blind."

—Phases: *Poet, Priest, Prostitute, Politician, Scientist.*

16. (BRING) ORDER OGP: "To bring order to society and be supported in this or I will torture (burn?) their bodies (flesh?)."

—Phases: *Lawmaker, Criminal, Merchant, Priestess, Nurse.*

19. GUIDE OGP: "To guide settlers and have them respect me or I will burn it all down."

—Phases: *Scout, Wagonleader, Salesman*

(Trader), Lover (Frontier Girl), Little Girl.

21. CONSTRUCT OGP: "To construct spiral staircases and have them admired or I will trap them all."

—Phases: *Carpenter, Scornful Person, Salesman, Art Critic, Sexy Girl.*

24. STRUCTURE OGP: "To structure reality and be worshiped as a god or I will destroy them all."

—Phases: *Savior, Priest, Prostitute, General, Temple Virgin.*

33. ENLIGHTEN OGP: "To preach goodness and keep them from sin or else I will torture them."

—Phases: *Minister (?), Sinner, Ruler, Conqueror, (?).*

34. CONVERT OGP: "To convert unbelievers and make them (honest?) or I will implant them to believe."

—Phases: *Priest, Scoffer, Messenger (of the gods?), Empress, (?).*

45. GROW OGP: "To grow flowers and have them make people feel good or I

will sacrifice everyone."

—Phases: *Priestess, Policeman, Carpenter, Mother, Priest.*

46. DISCOVER OGP: "To discover truth.. and?"

—Phases: *(?)*

47. HEAL OGP: "To heal illness and receive the peoples' gratitude or I will make their bodies rot away."

—Phases: *Healer, Priest, Politician, Policeman, Priestess.*

51. UNITE OGP: "To unite the workers in building wondrous projects or I will trick them all into slavery forever."

—Phases: *Engineer, (?), Politician, (?), (?).*

54. COOPERATE OGP: "To get people to cooperate in maintaining society and become famous for doing this or I will betray everyone."

—Phases: *Policeman, Criminal, Lawmaker, Priest, Prostitute.*

55. PARTICIPATE OGP: "To participate in dancing and be admired for my beauty

of form or else I will cut their hearts out."

—Phases: *Dancer, Critic, Father, Innocent Girl, Lover.*

56. EXPAND OGP: "To expand knowledge and be admired for my genius or I will blow them all up."

—Phases: *Scientist, Priest, Psychiatrist, Girl, Ruler.*

57. REPRODUCE OGP: "To reproduce fine books and have the quality admired or I will inject them all with insanity (with a drug)."

—Phases: *Scribe (Scholar), Peasant, Scientist (Professor), Wife (Lover), Carpenter.*

58. SATISFY OGP: "To satisfy conventions and be respected or I will poison them all."

—Phases: *Girl, Elder Woman, Father, Lover, Publisher.*

59. JOIN OGP: "To join people together and have them be thankful for my help

or I will throw things at them."

—Phases: *Prophet, Businessman, Priest, Lawmaker, Inventor.*

60. CARE (FOR) OGP: "To care for children (and keep them safe) and be loved for it or I will claw everyone's eyes out."

—Phases: *(?)*

61. FEEL OGP: "To feel alive and gain everyone's agreement or I will drive them all crazy."

—Phases: *Athlete, Lawmaker, Coach, Lawyer, Professor.*

62. REPLENISH OGP: "To replenish the wildlife and be praised for restoring the planet or I will take it away from them."

—Phases: *Ecologist, Businessman, Housewife, Politician, Priest.*

63. EAT OGP: "To eat people and gain strength from their 'souls' or I will rend their 'souls' forever."

—Phases: *Cannibal, Enemies, Lover, Priest,*

Explorer.

64. ENDURE OGP: "To endure existence and be left alone or I will enslave them all."
— Phases: *Carpenter, Juvenile Delinquent, Wife, Detective, Salesman(?).*

After the basic (positive) Goals, this continues with the *inversions* (*negative-Goals run in the reverse Goals-Sequence order*).

INV 59. SEPARATE OGP: "To separate people from groups and be praised for helping them or I will leave forever."
— Phases: *Messiah, Ruler, Ruler's Mistress, General, Slave Girl.*

INV 58. RIDICULE OGP: "To ridicule social conventions and have everyone amused by this or I will hide forever."
— Phases: *Publisher, Father, Lover, Girl, Elder Woman.*

INV 54. INVALIDATE OGP: "To get people to individuate from groups which exploit them and have them feel good that I did this or I will shoot myself."

—Phases: *Prostitute, Priest, Criminal, Lawmaker, Politician.*

INV 48. ROT OGP: "To rot other's minds and make them suggestible or I will dissipate myself."

—Phases: *Salesman, Professor, Politician, Judge, Girl.*

INV 29. PERVERT OGP: "To pervert little children and have all the parents fear me or I will hang myself forever."

—Phases: *Pornographer, Judge (Moralist), Publisher, Parents, Little Girl.*

INV 16. (BRING) CHAOS OGP: "To bring chaos and overwhelm everybody or I will hide myself away forever."

—Phases: *Dark Priest (Black Magician), Criminal (?), Lawmaker (?), Prostitute (?), Temple Virgin (?).*

INV 4. DISILLUSION OGP: "To disillusion writers and force society to accept my judgment or I will bash my head in."

—Phases: *Critic, Writer, Father, Publisher, Actor.*

INV 3X. DRAIN OGP: "To drain emotion and make everyone apathetic or I will dissipate myself/others forever."

—Phases: *Artisan (craftsman), Scientist, Fishmonger, Policeman, Priest.*

INV 1. DESTROY OGP: "To destroy all of creation and be worshiped or I will uncreate myself/others forever."

—Phases: *Devil, God, Worshipers, Artisan, Virgin.*

THE "BIG-SPLITTER" INCIDENT
(*Advanced Technical Research*)

This final section of our *advanced training* program presents the experimental research (and procedures) for handling the "*Big Splitter Implant.*" Best we can determine at this time: this is the "*entry-*

into-the-Symbols-Universe"-incident.

We know this occurs after an *Alpha-Spirit* had already experienced *"The Treadmill"* in the *Games-Universe*. [The *Big-Splitter* is constructed to restimulate elements of *The Treadmill*.]

This section includes a new standard procedure. However, for training purposes, we also include the prior research and experimental procedures for this *Implant*. The material has not yet been refined for a standard presentation. This means much of the written background data and explanation still appears with the prior experimental versions, and a *Seeker* should study *all* of its parts before applying anything from this section.

While originally researching and applying earlier versions of this work, we did not yet have the *"Locational Procedure"* (*AT#5*). As a result, *defragmentation* of *"split-fragments"* required many additional steps that the new standard procedure does not. This makes the new standard seem like an oversimplification—but it *is* effective if a *Seeker* understands the true nature of what they are handling with it. Older procedures and background data are included to assist this. [Older methods are still effective; but often more complex.]

During the *"Big Splitter"* *incident*, an *Alpha-Spirit* is made to *split-off* (*fragment*) into *128* types of *entities*, each of which has various functions—such as keeping the *Universe* manifested, or blocking perception, *&tc*. The *Implant-pattern* was repeated multiple times, using each of the IPU-*Goals*. This means we have a lot of *fragmented-pieces* of ourselves *being* these various things. [A *Seeker* should *disperse* some accessible surface *charge* from the *Implanted Penalty-Universes* (*AT#4*) prior to treating this section (if they have not already).] *New Standard "Entity-Handling"* includes:

A. Using the list of *128-entity types*: check the type of *entity* for a *Meter-read* and *spot* where it is; or *spot* one that is *being* this type.

B. *Locational Procedure.* [*AT#5*] Have the *entity* "point to the being" it "divided from." At *Wizard-Levels*, this is usually sufficient to *disperse* or *release* the *entity* (*split-fragment*). You may have to get it to *point* a few times until it gets its own certainty. It doesn't matter "where" it's pointing, or if *you* are certain about it; it is the *entity* that requires certainty in order to *release* itself. If necessary, apply the next step.

C. *Identification Procedure.* [*AT#5*] If necessary, have the *entity* "Identify" itself properly by applying the "*Who Are You?*"-PCL (getting the "*me*" answer), until it *disperses* or *releases*.

D. Check again and repeat A-to-C until no more *entities* are responding for that type.

Go through the entire *entity-type-list* from top to bottom, handling anything that reacts—and not working too hard at trying to "wake" a lot up. When you have completed with *running* one cycle through the *list*: start at the top and go through it again. Repeat this until the whole *list* is *defragmented* (doesn't *register*).

After working with the *New Standard* method, a *Seeker* can use the previously researched methods (given later) to see if any more *entities* are "awakened" (show up) for *processing*. It is quite possible that some of the earlier experimental methods are still necessary for *total defragmentation* of this area, which is another reason we have retained them in this manual (in addition to educating about progressive research).

You could apply the full *Splitter-Platform*, using the most basic (first) IPU-*Goal*—"*To Create*"—and then *run* the above steps again, this time going much deeper (un-

less you have already hit the main structure of it and taken the whole thing
apart).

This final area we are treating in this final training manual might actually be
able to be *run* all the way toward a point
of major *realization/recognition* that
handles *all* of the *split-fragments* of yourself. As yet, no one (within our organiza-
tion that we know of) has taken this
work to such an ultimate *end-point.*

One of the final activities an individual
theoretically conducts prior to a true
"Wizard Level-8 Ascension" is the *re-collec-*
tion of all *split-fragments* present in the
Universe; because an *Alpha-Spirit* must
get out "in wholeness," without any
lingering attachments or connectivity to
this Physical Universe. Otherwise a "part"
of us would still remain, and we would
not be truly free to manifest or locate our
Awareness fully on some other plane.

If any of our fixed *"anchor-points"* remain here, we could just as easily be "snapped back in" to this *reality*; or "collapse-in to" it, when it too, one day, collapses-in on the next lower condensation of *agreements*.

If you miss (*fly past*) an *entity* of the type that you're checking that is ready for *processing* and try to continue, you may not find anything on the *next* type—even though the *next* type isn't really cleared. In this case, go back and check the *previous* type (you had just been working with) again for *flown-by fragments.*

This is all best handled with a *Biofeedback-device.* A lot of these *fragments* are off in "*non-physical locations*," so a *Seeker* should not limit their *attention* to what is only in the immediate area of the Body (as with B.E., *&tc.*) or become overly concerned with "*where*" these *locations* actually are.

SPLITTER-INCIDENT ENTITY-TYPES

This is a list of the *128 entity* types resulting from the *"Big Splitter" incident* (which occurs using the *Splitter-Platform* that is given later). We have the *Platform* developed. The real goal of all experimental procedures (in this area) is to undercut having to *run* the entire *Platform* several times on each of the *128* types.

This list provides the *entity* types in the *reverse* order from how they occur in the *incident*; because that is the easiest way to *run* them when using the *Wizard-Level* ability of *"dispersing-on-realization/Awareness"* (as is the case with the *New Standard* methods). Otherwise, a *Seeker* will have to *process-out* all of the *"programming items"* that are found in the *Platform* for each type.

Note that we have a *"translation"* issue with ascribing *"human language"* names to represent these various types. Usually this is not an issue so long as a *Seeker* has no misconception about what a word means. In this case, we are working toward defining *"type labels"* that are consistent when checking for *Meter-reads*.

There are *16* groups or classes of *entity*; each of which has *8* types. Alternative *labels* appear for some types; the result of different researchers working on this project at different experimental periods of development.

GROUP 16. FINAL BARRIERS (*Blockages against taking this Implant apart.*)

128. OVERSOUL (manages all the others)
127. GUARDIAN (guards the implant against erasure)
126. HOLDER (holds entities in place that try to release)
125. SUPPRESSOR (hides the implant)
  125x. HIDER (may be 'suppressor')
124. DENIER (says implant never happened)
123. MISDIRECTOR (alters and shifts attention)

123x. **BOUNCER** ('misdirector')

122. **INVALIDATOR** (invalidates anything you run/process)

121. **RESTIMULATOR** (keeps the implant restimulated)

121x. **RESISTOR** (resists change)

GROUP 15. FINAL STRUCTURE (*Entities maintaining the structure of Implant.*)

120. **UNIFIER** (pulls everything together)

120x. **JOINER** or **GROUPER**

119. **KEEPER** (keeps/holds you down in the implant)

118. **IMPLANTER** (continually runs implant-items on you)

117. **SPLITTER** (continually makes everyone split/divide/fragment)

116. **CORRECTIVE ENTITY** (fixes anything that becomes undone)

116x. **REPAIRER**

115. **PERPETUATOR** (keeps the implant going)

114. **DRAMATIZER**

113. **INNER GUARD** (keeps you from

looking at yourself and seeing the structure of the implant/entities)

GROUP 14. SPIRITUAL BARRIERS (*Blocks*)

112. DEVIL (DEMON) (makes trouble for you)

111. DEGRADER (encourages degradation)

110. TEMPTER (tempts you to do evil)

109. DELUSION ENTITY (creates delusions)

108. TERROR (FEAR) ENTITY (makes you afraid; particularly involving the Mind or Spirits)

107. CONFUSION ENTITY (tries to keep you confused)

106. DISCOURAGER (discourages any effort to do anything about this)

105. INTERIORIZER (makes you 'interiorize'; into Universes and bodies, *&tc.*)

GROUP 13. SPIRITUAL STRUCTURE

104. RECYCLER (cycles you into a 'new'

beingness between lives)

103. **EXECUTIONER** (destroys your 'old' identity between lives)

102. **PUNISHER** (arranges punishments)

101. **JUDGE** (harshly judges your conduct, particularly between lives)

101x. **BETWEEN-LIVES ENTITY** (?)

100. **ACCUSER** (accuses you of any possible wrongdoing)

99. **ATTRACTOR** (causes you to 'pull' things in)

98. **ANGEL** (a piece of yourself sent to serve 'god'/'Universal Mind')

97. **CREATOR / PART-OF-GOD** (a part of yourself sent to be part of 'god'; or contribution to the 'Universal Mind'; "to be the thought of the Universe forever," &tc.)

97x. **UNIVERSAL-MIND** (likely the same as 97)

[Note that the "*god*" or "*Universal Mind*" that is set up by this *Implant* is *Universe*-managing *machinery* and not a "*Self-*

aware entity" in the conventional sense. It is composed of a piece of everyone and is programmed like a computer to run *reality* in the *Universe*. This should not be confused with any "higher dynamic" idea of "*god*" or "*Source*." Part of us makes up the *Universal-Mind* ("*god*") and part is made into an "*angel*" that runs around enacting *god's* orders.]

GROUP 12. EXISTENCE BARRIERS (*Blocks*)

96. TRICKSTER (tricks you)
95. FATE (ARRANGER) (arranges fates for you)
94. DISPERSER (disperses you)
93. INVERTER (turns your postulates back against you)
92. DECEIVER (deceives you)
91. OPPOSER (manifests opposition to your goals)
90. EQUALIZER (balances things; arranges 'karma')
89. WATCHER (watches you)

GROUP 11. EXISTENCE STRUCTURE

88. ALIGNER (COORDINATOR)

87. COACH (keeps you from either winning or losing)

  87x. HUMANIZER

86. ENCOURAGER (encourages you to stay here and live life)

85. FUTURIZER (puts things into the future for you)

84. GOAL-MAKER (manifests goals for you)

83. GAME-MAKER (manifests games for you)

82. PLANNER (plans your continued existence)

81. GUIDE (guides you deeper/further into existence/Universe)

GROUP 10. UNIVERSE BARRIERS (*Blocks*)

80. REFLECTOR (ENERGY MIRROR) (unmanifests energy-beams by reflecting them back at you)

  80x. COLLAPSAR

79. VACUUM (UNMANIFESTOR) (drains

energy and energy-beams)

78. PULL-BACK (causes you to pull back your energy-beams)

78x. BEAM-STOPPER

77. DIFFUSER (causes energy-beams to disperse and slide off targets)

77x. DEFLECTOR (likely same as 77)

76. CONSTRAINER (constrains you to follow 'physical laws')

75. BLOCKER (blocks you from messing up structure of Universe)

74. BINDER (binds you together with reality-agreements)

74x. AGREEMENT-ENTITY

73. PROTECTOR (protects Universe from your postulates)

73x. UNIVERSE-HOLDER

GROUP 9. UNIVERSE STRUCTURE

72. ACTUALIZER (makes it all real)

72x. SOLIDIFIER or PERSISTER

71. SYNCHRONIZER (cross-copies the simultaneousness of time between individuals)

70. UNIVERSE COORDINATOR
(coordinates the interrelationship of
space-time and energy-matter)

69. DETERMINATOR (judges value of
potential futures in order to maximize
'Arcs of Infinity')

68. COMMUNICATOR (interconnects
everyone)

67. LOCATOR (maintains the position of
everything)

66. GENERATOR (projects reality)

65. POSTULATOR (manifests reality)

GROUP 8. SOCIAL/LIFE BARRIERS
(*Blocks*)

64. SINNER (inspires 'sin', selfishness,
&tc.)

63. CONFLICTOR (inspires conflict)

62. SEXUAL ENTITY (sensation and
exchange of entities during sex, *&tc.*)

61. SUBLIMATING ENTITY (feelings of
love, honor, courage, loyalty, *&tc.*)

60. MOOD ENTITY (shifts moods
between extremes; serene/troubled,

calm/nervous, pleasant/irritated, *&tc.*)

59. **EMOTIONAL ENTITY** ('Beta-Awareness'; feelings of cheerfulness, boredom, antagonism, rage, hostility, fear, grief, apathy, *&tc.*)

58. **ATTITUDE ENTITY** (manifests preference; 'likes'/'dislikes', *&tc.*)

57. **MORALIZER** (makes you feel guilty)

GROUP 7. SOCIAL/LIFE STRUCTURE

56. **MISOWNER** (says that the Universe is not your creation so you can't affect it)

55. **SHELL (FOCAL)** (surrounds you and focuses things in on you)

54. **UNIVERSE LIFE-ENTITY** (to be 'the life' in the Universe)

53. **ANIMATOR** (to be 'the life' in lower organisms)

52. **SYMPATHIZER** (to keep you in sympathy)

51. **SOCIAL ENTITY** (inspires communication, agreement, likingness, *&tc.*)

50. **GROUP-MIND** (to be in 'groups')

49. **SUPER-BEING** (says you evolve by overwhelming individuals and making all become one)

GROUP 6. BODY BARRIERS (*Blocks*)

48. **SICKNESS ENTITY** (manifests disease according to 'universe laws')

47. **JAILER** (keeps you in a body)

46. **SLEEP-CENTER** (dreams; has you rebuild/manifest things while you sleep)

45. **SOMATIC-ENTITY** (manages physical pains/sensations)

44. **BODY-BLOCKER** (keeps you from modifying the body by postulate)

44x. **PERCEPTION-BLOCKER**

43. **FILTER** (filters out perception of entities, infinities, *&tc.*)

42. **CRAVER** (initiates cravings; food, *&tc.*)

41. **COMPELLER** (needing bodies; needing food, *&tc.*, for bodies)

41x. **COMPULSIVE ENTITY**

GROUP 5. BODY STRUCTURE

40. **RELAYER** (relays body perceptions to you)

39. **REPRESENTER** (manifests body perceptions; sight, *&tc.*)

   39x. **VISUAL-ENTITY** (composes pictures of reality that you look at instead of seeing it directly)

38. **REACTIVE ENTITY** (generates body reactions to environmental stimuli)

37. **BODY MACHINE** (regulates organic body processes)

36. **CELLULAR ENTITY** (creates/duplicates cells of the body)

35. **BODY-LOCATOR** (integrates cells, perceptions, *&tc.*, with space-time positions)

34. **GENETIC-ENTITY** (manages the body as a vehicle)

33. **BODY-GENERATOR** (projects the body into reality/Universe)

GROUP 4. MIND BARRIERS (*Blocks*)

32. **SHIFTER** (shifts attention into 'Beta-

Existence' and off of 'Alpha')

31. CONSCIENCE
30. JUSTIFIER
29. FORGETTER
28. ENTURBULATOR
27. DEPRESSOR (possibly related to *106*)
26. EXHILARATOR
25. CONTROLLER

GROUP 3. MIND STRUCTURE

24. FILE CLERK (retrieves data)
23. RECORDING-ENTITY
  23x. HISTORIAN
22. SYMBOLIZER
21. COMPUTATIONAL ENTITY
20. DECISION-MAKER
19. RANDOMIZER
18. THINKER
17. INSTIGATOR

GROUP 2. ALPHA-SPIRIT BLOCKERS

16. DESTROYER (arranges accidents, *&tc.*, to keep you from finding out about this, or escaping)

15. **NARCOTIC ENTITY** (keeps the 'Higher Self' feeling drugged)

14. **INHIBITOR** (blocks non-physical perception, *&tc.*)

13. **DAMPER (DAMPENER)** (keeps you condensed to a single point and in agreement, *&tc.*; holds you down)

12. **PREVENTER** (prevents manipulation of probability, resonance, cohesion, *&tc.*)

11. **WRAITH** (drains energy)

10. **SUBCONSCIOUS** (hides things; convinces you to stay limited and obedient)

9. **ABERRATOR** (compels one to follow laws of 'cumulative charge', fragmented patterns, restimulation, *&tc.*)

GROUP 1. ALPHA STRUCTURING

8. **FORMULATOR** (inspires choices of strength/weakness, likes/dislikes, *&tc.*)

7. **INSPIRATIONAL ENTITY** (inspires

beliefs that everyone likes it here and you wouldn't want to leave, &tc.)

6. SEPARATOR (keeps you as an individual separate from 'Higher Self', and from knowing about other entities, infinities, &tc.)

5. RESTRICTOR (limits awareness to a located viewpoint)

4. INDIVIDUALIZER (limits you to a single located viewpoint, beingness, &tc.)

3. BENEFACTOR (gives you interesting rewards, &tc., for obeying the implant)

2. MANIFESTATION-INVALIDATOR (invalidates anything that is not 'agreed-upon')

2x. CREATION-MOCKUP INVALIDATOR

1. INITIATOR (compels you to desire 'agreed-upon' Universe; games, forms, reality, existence, &tc.)

THE "HIGHER SELF" H.S. PROCEDURE
(Archaic Splitter-Handling Tech., Revised)

This advanced experimental-research method is based on the concept of a *"Higher-Self"* being established for each of the IPU-*Goals*. These "higher selves" are unaware (compartmented) pieces of yourself that keep everything manifested and operating. [This method is not necessarily recommended. It is a record of the material we utilized for research prior to the *New Standard* techniques, with the "locational procedure," &tc.]

Terminology for this application emerged from the idea of a *"Higher Self"* and that if such an entity or part of us is really fragmented and separated (compartmented), than we had to ask ourselves: *"higher" than what?* Handling IPU-material and other techniques for *Implanting-Incidents* has run us up to *this* point—theoretically the final major "barrier" (or "level of work") that keeps us from *Ascending out of this Universe.*

The IPU-*Goal* for the *H.S. Procedure* is selected by assessment. A *Seeker* doesn't have to worry about *running* a specific *Goal-sequence*; they assess for what currently gives the largest *Meter-reads* and *run* that. The procedure really has two parts: one, is the actual *running* of the *"higher self"* items; and two, is the handling of *8* types of *blocking-entities* that interfere with *processing-out* this *Implant*.

Although *128 entity types* are installed by the *Splitter Platform*, only one bunch of *8* seem to interfere specifically with *systematic processing* (*defragmenting*). You *process* the *8 blocking-entities* whenever you start your session for the day, and if necessary, in between each pass through the *"higher self"* items on a particular IPU-*Goal*; and also if you run into interference that is keeping *items* from *dispersing/defragmenting.*

The *"higher self"* programming-items are defragmented as a batch or cluster; not as individual *line-items*. You just *spot* one after another and keep going through the entire batch of *programming-items* until they collectively do not *register.* Trying to *defrag* line-by-line seems to stir up too much opposition to *dispersal*.

[*Researcher Notes*: If a *Seeker* runs into a *GSR-Meter* phenomenon where the needle is "slamming": there are likely *Harmful-Acts* connected to whatever is being handled, which need to be *spotted/ defragged.* If the *balance-point* on the *Meter* is excessively high (*high-resistance reading*), handle only *blocking-entities* until it lowers. When the "*higher self*" items do *register* as *erased/dispersed*, then they are. Don't *overrun*. There is a distinct feeling of the *Universe* shifting around when one of the "*higher selves*" disperses.]

BLOCKING-ENTITIES LIST

Use this *list* for assessment:

  GUARDIAN
  OVERSOUL

HOLDER
SUPPRESSOR
DENIER
MISDIRECTOR
INVALIDATOR
RESTIMULATOR

Whenever you get a *Meter-read*, have the *entity* do the following:

A. *"Spot being made into a(n) ___."*

B. *"Spot being made to split."*

 [*Revision*: add *Locational Proc.* here.]

C. *"Spot the first time you were made to split."*

D. *"Spot making others split."*

E. If necessary: *Identification Proc.* (*"Who Are You?"*/*"Me"*)

At this level of work, you may get an early *dispersal/release* of an *entity* without realizing it, and start *processing* another of the same type that was behind the first one. But since the second one didn't get the first-PCL (*&tc.*) or whatever the first *released* on, there is still something there

178

by STEP-E. So, if something remains, check if you're handling another of the same type; and if so, go back to STEP-A. In any case, when one does *release*, you check for another of the same type.

H.S. PROCEDURE

A. *Spot "Native State" line-item for the Goal. Spot* being *pushed-in — pushing others in*; and *another pushing others in* —to the *Implanted Penalty-Universe* (IPU) for this *Goal*.

B. *Spot* the *item*: "TO {*goal*} IS TO BE THE INFINITE {*terminal*} AND DIVIDE INTO MY HIGHER AND LOWER SELF FOREVER."

C. *Spot* being the *"higher self"* as a manifestation of the "infinite {*terminal*}." Repeat STEP-A (*Native State*) from the *"higher self"* viewpoint.

D. From the *"higher self"* viewpoint: *Spot* the original *split* into the "infinite {*terminal*}." *Spot* the "mirror" that shows you *splitting* into *infinite-copies* of the *terminal*; and *spot* becoming the *terminal* spread out to *infinity*.

[*Revision*: add *Locational Proc.* here on "higher self" viewpoint.]

E. *Process* the *"higher self"* through the following *"programming items."* Make sure each *item* gives a *Meter-read* (contacting it), but don't continue to *defrag* each line. [See earlier instruction on this.] If you can't get an *item* to *register,* check if it has been "*sup pressed*" or "*invalidated*." If the *Meter-needle* goes dead, or gets "stuck," check for *blocking-entities*.

The *H.S. programming-items*:

TO {goal} INFINITELY IS TO BE MY HIGHER-SELF AND ___.
1. CREATE THIS FOREVER
2. DEFEND THIS FOREVER
3. REPLACE THIS FOREVER
4. KEEP THIS MANIFESTED FOREVER
5. ESTABLISH THIS SPACE FOREVER

6. HIDE THIS FOREVER
7. HOLD THIS TOGETHER FOREVER
8. KEEP THIS UNCHANGING FOREVER
9. MAINTAIN THIS LOCATION FOREVER
10. ENERGIZE THIS FOREVER
11. PROTECT THIS FOREVER
12. OBSCURE THIS FOREVER
13. SOLIDIFY THIS FOREVER
14. STABILIZE THIS FOREVER
15. GUARD THIS FOREVER
16. FORGET THIS FOREVER

SPLITTER-INCIDENT (& PLATFORM)

This is the original research-data for the *"Big-Splitter" Implanting-Incident* used for early experiments. It was first replaced by *H.S. Procedure* and then, more recently, by the *New Standard* method. However, the details included in this original research are reissued any time the material is revised to avoid rewriting them. This is also such a key area of *Ascension* that all existing records of this work are considered critical for posterity.

[The actual *incident-sequence* is given as "capital-lettered" *items*, such as "TO {*goal*}.." There are also various *"spotting"* instructions included for *contacting-the-incident*, research and *defragmentation*.]

SECTION 1. INFINITY
(*The space is like being in a thin white cloud with nothing visible.*)

A. TO {*goal*} INFINITELY IS TO:
1. PERCEIVE ULTIMATE TRUTH
2. ACHIEVE ULTIMATE PURPOSE
3. PERCEIVE ULTIMATE BEAUTY
4. EXPERIENCE ULTIMATE ENLIGHTENMENT
5. RECEIVE ULTIMATE ADMIRATION
6. ACHIEVE ULTIMATE BEINGNESS
7. ACHIEVE ULTIMATE DOINGNESS
8. ACHIEVE ULTIMATE HAVINGNESS
9. WIELD ULTIMATE POWER
10. BE GOD

B. THE TEMPLE
1. *Spot:* The {*terminal*} appears in front of you.

2. TO {*goal*} IS TO BECOME THE INFINITE {*terminal*}:
3. TO BECOME THE INFINITE {*terminal*} IS TO BECOME GOD
4. *Spot:* The *temple* appears in front of you.
5. TO BECOME GOD IS TO BECOME THE INFINITE {*terminal*} AND DO {*goal*} INFINITELY

C. SPOTTING STEPS

(*Spot* the following PCL with *intention;* then broadcast it out to the *entities, &tc.,* that started waking up from *running* the above steps.)

1. "*Spot the false data (above) in the Implant.*"
2. "*Spot that you don't have to be the terminal to do the goal.*"
3. "*Spot that you don't have to do the goal to get the things promised (above).*"
4. "*Spot that you don't have to be the terminal to get the things promised (above).*"
5. "*Spot that these items were all false promises; and that you didn't get these*

things from obeying the Implant."

D. ENTITY-PROCESSING

(*Broadcast* the following PCL out to *process* awakened *entities, &tc.*)

1. *"Spot being made to divide by this Implant."*

[*Revision*: add *Locational Proc.* here.]

2. *"Spot the first time you were made to divide; Spot making others divide."*

3. *"Spot the false data in the Implant; Spot the first time you were implanted with false data."*

4. *"Spot being made to copy; Spot the first time you were made to copy; Spot making others copy."*

5. *"Spot: 'To {goal} is Native State' at the top of the original Implanted Penalty-Universe Platform; Spot being pushed into it; pushing another into it; and others pushing others into it."*

6. *"Come up to present time. Thank You."*

Check for individual *entities/fragments* remaining.

[*Revision*: use *Locational* and *Identificat-*

ion Tech with acknowledgments.] Check for, and handle, any *Guardians*, *machinery*, and/or other *entity* types.

SECTION 2. INFINITE TERMINAL

(*The items from the first section are reused with the "Infinite Terminal" in place of the Goal, as follows. While the items are given, the terminal—which is facing you—drifts backward toward "the Temple" and through the entrance. You are drawn along by it and enter "the Temple" as well.*)

A. TO BECOME THE INFINITE {*terminal*} IS TO: {*items 1 through 10 of Section-1A*}

B. (*The terminal is floating in the center of "the Temple" facing you.*) TO BE GOD IS TO CHOOSE TO BE THE INFINITE {*terminal*} AND DO {*goal*} INFINITELY

C. (*You slide into the manifestation of the terminal. You do this by curving around to the right and sliding in on the terminal's left side—so you are now facing toward the direction you just were in and are now*

*looking through the terminal's viewpoint. As
this happens, you get the following item.
Also: Spot the feeling of turning and sliding
into the terminal as you spot the item. There
is a heavy emphasis on the word 'Be'.)*

TO {goal} **IS TO BE THE** {terminal}

*D. Spot seeing the inside of "the Temple"
from the terminal's eyes (viewpoint). Notice
that everything looked vague and dreamlike
before, but now looks solid and sharp-looking
with the terminal's eyes (viewpoint). This is
a part of the trick/gimmick of the Implant-
Universe. You were actually perceiving
correctly before. Spot this trick happening.*

*E. Notice that there is some type of mirror
on a wall of "the Temple"; and you can see
yourself in it as the terminal. Spot the mirror.
Spot the false reflection of yourself as the
terminal.*

*F. (With this item, the mirror shows you
splitting out to infinity.)*

**TO BECOME GOD IS TO BECOME
INFINITE**

(Endless copies of the terminal stream out in all directions. Actually, you are being shown a picture of the terminal splitting, but you think you are already splitting and start agreeing with the idea. Then you are hit with a wave of force that makes you split. Spot the false mirror image, and the wave of force, along with the item.)

G. *(With this item, the mirror view pans backwards and shows you the outside of "the Temple" with endless copies of the terminal streaming off in all directions. Spot this.)*

TO {*goal*} IS TO DIVIDE FOREVER

H. TO {*goal*} IS TO BE THE INFINITE {*terminal*}

I. The original procedure includes: *imagining* dividing out to infinity and being the "*infinite-terminal*" several times. Also: have any *entities* (*&tc.*) that are awake "*spot*" doing this; and *spot* the first time they did this.

J. A revised procedure includes: alternate *running* the conceptual-PCL "*Decide*

To Be The Infinite {terminal}" and *"Decide Not To Be The Infinite {terminal}."* (Always end on the second one.)

K. Repeat *"Entity-Processing"* (STEP-D from *Section-1*).

L. **TO** {goal} **IS TO BE THE INFINITE** {terminal} **AND:** {items 1 through 16 of Step-E of the H.S. Procedure}

For the *remaining* sections (below): *spot* the *item* a number of times until it *releases, disperses* or stops *registering*; have anyone awake *spot* doing the *item* (and the first time); and then *spot* the *item* again to *disperse* or to confirm *release/defrag.*

The original version includes: *spot* being the *infinite-copies* of the *terminal* and doing the *item* yourself (to be at total *Cause* over doing the *item*); then *spot* the *item* and the *"Native State"* item for that Goal.

SECTION 3. INFINITE REALITY

(A feeling of something shifting or coming apart almost always means dispersion/defrag-

mentation. Total defragmentation does not give quite the same feeling as a partial-release. The shift on a full dispersal/release basically feels good; you are shifting back towards reality, and you feel better oriented. Partial-releases tend to leave one feeling disoriented.)

TO {*goal*} IS TO BE THE INFINITE {*terminal*} AND PARTICIPATE IN THE:

1. CO-ACTUALIZATION OF REALITY, FOREVER
2. SHARING OF GROUP AGREEMENT, FOREVER
3. RHYTHM OF AGREED-UPON TIME, FOREVER
4. DETERMINATION OF AGREED-UPON LOCATION, FOREVER
5. OPERATION OF PHYSICAL UNIVERSE MECHANICS/LAWS, FOREVER
6. ENERGIZATION OF AGREED-UPON MOTION, FOREVER
7. SOLIDIFICATION OF AGREED-UPON FORMS, FOREVER
8. CROSS-COPYING OF THE PHYSICAL UNIVERSE, FOREVER

SECTION 4. SPLIT & PROGRAMMING

There are 128 entity-types. The first item for each is the "split" into that type. Something like a drop of water appears and then breaks apart and fragments into endless tiny droplets spreading across space-time. Spot this with the item.

The second item is a "program" item. The infinite droplets of water freeze or crystallize. Spot this with the item.

This sequence is introduced with:

0.0 TO {*goal*} IS TO BE THE INFINITE {*terminal*} AND

0.1 COPY MYSELF AND OTHERS, FOREVER

0.2 DIVIDE MYSELF AND OTHERS, FOREVER

A *"split/program"* pattern occurs with the *first two items* for each *entity* type. After all the *items/entities*, there is an additional H.S. *item* (after a repeat of *item* 0.0 above) as follows:

129.0 DIVIDE MYSELF INTO MY HIGHER SELF AND MYSELF AS AN INDIVIDUAL, FOREVER

Then there are eight different "doingness" programming-items for each type. It is easier to run these for each entity type along with the "split-program" items (above), rather than making a separate cycle through for these details.

A revised handling of the "doingness" programming-items includes imagining doing (and not doing) the action, alternately to an end-realization or end-point. Once this is clearly conceived, then broadcast processing to entities: spot being made into (type), and the first time, and making others; use "Locational Tech" (point to..); spot false data of the Implant; spot "Native State" item; and apply "Identification Tech," &tc. —all as needed to resolve the case.

[Note that some additional data (research and experimentation) is still necessary to fully complete this final step toward *Ascension*.]

1.1 SPLIT MYSELF AND OTHERS INTO INITIATORS FOREVER

1.2 PROGRAM MYSELF AND OTHERS TO BE THE INITIATOR AND INFUSE MYSELF WITH DESIRE FOREVER

1.X TO {*goal*} INFINITELY IS TO BE THE INITIATOR AND COMPEL MYSELF TO DESIRE PHYSICAL UNIVERSE ___, FOREVER

[1. TIME; 2. SPACE; 3. ENERGY; 4. MATTER; 5. GAMES; 6. FORMS; 7. REALITY; 8. EXISTENCE]

2.1 SPLIT MYSELF AND OTHERS INTO MOCK-UP INVALIDATORS FOREVER

2.2 PROGRAM MYSELF AND OTHERS TO BE THE MOCK-UP INVALIDATOR AND INVALIDATE THAT WHICH IS NOT AGREED-UPON, FOREVER

2.X TO {*goal*} INFINITELY IS TO BE THE MOCK-UP INVALIDATOR AND INVALIDATE NON-PHYSICAL ___ FOREVER

[1. TIME; 2. SPACE; 3. ENERGY; 4. MATTER; 5. GAMES; 6. FORMS; 7. REALITY; 8. EXISTENCE]

3.1 SPLIT MYSELF AND OTHERS INTO BENEFACTORS FOREVER

3.2 PROGRAM MYSELF AND OTHERS TO BE THE BENEFACTOR AND REWARD MYSELF FOR OBEYING THIS IMPLANT FOREVER

3.X TO {goal} INFINITELY IS TO BE THE BENEFACTOR AND GIVE MYSELF INTERESTING ___ TO OCCUPY MY ATTENTION FOREVER

[1. GOALS; 2. HAVINGNESS; 3. PHASES; 4. GAMES; 5. ADVENTURES; 6. DRAMA]

3.Y TO {goal} INFINITELY IS TO BE THE BENEFACTOR AND GIVE MYSELF INTERESTING ___ FOR OBEYING THIS FOREVER

[7. REASONS; 8. REWARDS]

4.1 SPLIT MYSELF AND OTHERS INTO INDIVIDUALIZERS FOREVER

4.2 PROGRAM MYSELF AND OTHERS TO BE THE INDIVIDUALIZER AND KEEP MYSELF NARROWED DOWN (or compartmented) FOREVER

4.X TO {goal} INFINITELY IS TO BE THE INDIVIDUALIZER AND ___ FOREVER

[1. SHIFT MY AWARENESS DOWN TO A POINT; 2. KEEP MYSELF LOCATED IN SPACE AND TIME]

4.Y   TO {goal} INFINITELY IS TO BE THE INDIVIDUALIZER AND LIMIT MYSELF TO A SINGLE ___ FOREVER

[3. VIEWPOINT; 4. AWARENESS CENTER; 5. TIME-TRACK; 6. OPERATING POINT; 7. BEINGNESS; 8. REALITY]

5.1   SPLIT MYSELF AND OTHERS INTO RESTRICTORS FOREVER

5.2   PROGRAM MYSELF AND OTHERS TO BE THE RESTRICTOR AND LIMIT MYSELF TO A LOCATED VIEWPOINT, FOREVER

5.X   TO {goal} INFINITELY IS TO BE THE RESTRICTOR AND RESTRICT MYSELF TO ___ ONLY IN THE LOCATED VIEWPOINT, FOREVER

[1. BEING; 2. PERCEIVING; 3. OPERATING; 4. THINKING]

5.X   TO {goal} INFINITELY IS TO BE THE RESTRICTOR AND RESTRICT MY ___ OF THE LOCATED VIEWPOINT, FOREVER

194

[5. CONCEPTIONS TO THE EXPERIENCE; 6. KNOWLEDGE TO THE DATA; 7. POWER TO THE ENERGY; 8. ABILITIES TO THE CAPABILITIES]

6.1 SPLIT MYSELF AND OTHERS INTO SEPARATORS FOREVER

6.2 PROGRAM MYSELF AND OTHERS TO BE THE SEPARATOR AND KEEP MYSELF SEPARATE AS AN INDIVIDUAL, FOREVER

6.X TO {goal} INFINITELY IS TO BE THE SEPARATOR AND KEEP MYSELF AS AN INDIVIDUAL, SEPARATE FROM ___, FOREVER

[1. MYSELF AS AN ENTITY; 2. MY HIGHER SELF; 3. INFINITY; 4. OTHER INDIVIDUALS; 5. OTHER UNIVERSES; 6. GOD (the unmanifest static or NOTHINGNESS); 7. THE LIFE STATIC (or ALPHA-SPIRIT); 8. THE UNIVERSE MACHINERY]

7.1 SPLIT MYSELF AND OTHERS INTO INSPIRATIONAL ENTITIES FOREVER

7.2 PROGRAM MYSELF AND OTHERS TO BE THE INSPIRATIONAL ENTITY AND

195

CONVINCE MYSELF TO BELIEVE
IN ALL THIS FOREVER

7.X TO {goal} INFINITELY IS TO BE
THE INSPIRATIONAL ENTITY
AND CONVINCE MYSELF AND
OTHERS THAT ___, FOREVER

[1. EVERYONE REALLY LIKES IT
HERE; 2. THIS IS THE ONLY REAL
UNIVERSE; 3. THERE WAS NOTHING
BEFORE THIS UNIVERSE; 4. IT IS
NECESSARY TO BE HERE; 5. YOU
CANNOT DO ANYTHING WITHOUT
OTHERS AGREEMENT; 6. POSTULATES
CANNOT AFFECT THE PHYSICAL
UNIVERSE; 7. NOBODY CAN EXIST
WITHOUT A PHYSICAL FORM; 8. WE
WANT TO BE THE EFFECT OF ALL THIS.]

8.1 SPLIT MYSELF AND OTHERS
INTO FORMULATORS FOREVER

8.2 PROGRAM MYSELF AND
OTHERS TO BE THE
FORMULATOR AND FORMULATE
MYSELF AS AN INDIVIDUAL
FOREVER

8.X TO {goal} INFINITELY IS TO BE
THE FORMULATOR AND INSPIRE
MYSELF TO CHOOSE ___,
FOREVER

[1. STRENGTHS AND WEAKNESSES;

2. LIKES AND DISLIKES; 3. ALLIES AND
ENEMIES; 4. HOPES AND FEARS; 5.
CONNECTIONS AND DISCONNECTIONS;
6. FREEDOMS AND CONSEQUENCES;
7. ABILITIES AND DISABILITIES; 8. (?)]

9.1 SPLIT MYSELF AND OTHERS
INTO ABERRATORS FOREVER

9.2 PROGRAM MYSELF AND
OTHERS TO BE THE
ABERRATOR AND ABERRATE
(FRAGMENT) MYSELF FOREVER

9.X TO {goal} INFINITELY IS TO BE
THE ABERRATOR AND COMPEL
MYSELF TO FOLLOW THE LAWS
OF ___, FOREVER

[1. CUMULATIVE CHARGE (later
incidents stack up on earlier ones);
2. RESTIMULATION; 3. FLOWS (inflow,
outflow); 4. THE DECLINING SPIRAL (of
beingness and condensation);
5. EXCHANGE; 6. OPPOSITION (creating
your own); 7. PULLING THINGS IN
(manifesting motivation for actions); 8.
RESISTANCE (becoming what you resist).]

10.1 SPLIT MYSELF AND OTHERS
INTO SUBCONSCIOUS ENTITIES
FOREVER

10.2 PROGRAM MYSELF AND

197

OTHERS TO BE THE
SUBCONSCIOUS AND GIVE
MYSELF ORDERS FOREVER

10.X TO {goal} INFINITELY IS TO BE
THE SUBCONSCIOUS AND ___,
FOREVER

[1. HIDE FROM MYSELF AS AN
INDIVIDUAL; 2. KEEP MYSELF AS AN
INDIVIDUAL UNCONSCIOUS OF THESE
MECHANISMS; 3. KEEP MYSELF AS AN
INDIVIDUAL OBEDIENT TO THE
COMMANDS OF THIS IMPLANT; 4. KEEP
MYSELF AS AN INDIVIDUAL OBEDIENT
TO THE LAWS OF THE PHYSICAL
UNIVERSE; 5. LIMIT MY SELF-
AWARENESS TO MYSELF AS THE
INDIVIDUAL; 6. CONVINCE MYSELF
THAT THE ONLY WAY TO EXIST IS TO
ACCEPT THESE LIMITATIONS; 7.
CONVINCE MYSELF THAT THE ONLY
WAY TO BE HAPPY IS TO ACCEPT
THESE LIMITATIONS; 8. CONVINCE
MYSELF THAT THE ONLY WAY TO BE
GOOD IS TO ACCEPT THESE
LIMITATIONS]

11.1 SPLIT MYSELF AND OTHERS
INTO WRAITHS FOREVER

11.2 PROGRAM MYSELF AND
OTHERS TO BE THE WRAITH

AND WEAKEN MYSELF
FOREVER

11.X TO {*goal*} INFINITELY IS TO BE
THE WRAITH AND MAKE
MYSELF GROW CONTINUALLY
___, FOREVER

[1. LESS INTELLIGENT; 2. LESS
POWERFUL; 3. LESS ABLE; 4. LESS
SKILLFUL; 5. LESS AWARE; 6. LESS
INTEGRATED; 7. LESS COMPETENT;
8. SMALLER]

12.1 SPLIT MYSELF AND OTHERS
INTO PREVENTERS FOREVER

12.2 PROGRAM MYSELF AND
OTHERS TO BE THE
PREVENTER AND PREVENT THE
MANIPULATION OF REALITY,
FOREVER

12.X TO {*goal*} INFINITELY IS TO BE
THE PREVENTER AND PREVENT
THE MANIPULATION OF ___,
FOREVER

[1. PROBABILITY; 2. RESONANCE
(vibration/sympathy); 3. COHESION (the
cohesion of the whole); 4. SYNCHRONIZA-
TION (solidity/frequency); 5. ORIENTATION
(dimensions); 6. BEINGNESS (identity of
spaces, objects, energies); 7. WILLING-
NESS (of spaces, objects, energies);

8. ORIGINAL IS-NESS (actual nature of things/reality)]

13.1 SPLIT MYSELF AND OTHERS INTO DAMPERS FOREVER

13.2 PROGRAM MYSELF AND OTHERS TO BE THE DAMPER AND HOLD MYSELF HERE FOREVER

13.X TO {*goal*} INFINITELY IS TO BE THE DAMPER AND ___ FOREVER

[1. KEEP MYSELF AT EFFECT; 2. HOLD MYSELF DOWN; 3. KEEP MYSELF LOCATED; 4. CONDENSE MYSELF TO A POINT; 5. KEEP MYSELF IN AGREEMENT; 6. CONSTRAIN MYSELF TO PHYSICAL REALITY; 7. CONSTRAIN MYSELF TO A SINGLE INDIVIDUALITY; 8. HIDE ALL OTHER BEINGNESS FROM MY INDIVIDUAL SELF]

14.1 SPLIT MYSELF AND OTHERS INTO INHIBITORS FOREVER

14.2 PROGRAM MYSELF AND OTHERS TO BE THE INHIBITOR AND INHIBIT PERCEPTIONS FOREVER

14.X TO {*goal*} INFINITELY IS TO BE THE INHIBITOR AND ___

FOREVER

[1. BLOCK ALL PERCEPTION OF INFINITY; 2. BLOCK ALL PERCEPTIONS BEYOND 3 DIMENSIONS; 3. BLOCK ALL PERCEPTIONS OF ENTITIES; 4. BLOCK ALL PERCEPTIONS OF OTHER'S IMAGINED CREATIONS (MOCK-UPS); 5. BLOCK ALL PERCEPTION OF OTHER UNIVERSES; 6. BLOCK ALL PERCEPTION IN NON-PHYSICAL DIRECTIONS; 7. BLOCK MYSELF AND OTHERS FROM REALIZING THAT THESE THINGS ARE THERE; 8. BLOCK MYSELF AND OTHERS FROM WANTING TO DO ANYTHING ABOUT THIS]

15.1 SPLIT MYSELF AND OTHERS INTO NARCOTIC ENTITIES FOREVER

15.2 PROGRAM MYSELF AND OTHERS TO BE THE NARCOTIC ENTITY AND KEEP MY HIGHER-SELF "DRUGGED" FOREVER

15.X TO {*goal*} INFINITELY IS TO BE THE NARCOTIC ENTITY AND KEEP MY HIGHER-SELF ___ FOREVER

[1. LOST IN A FEELING OF PLEAS-ANT DRIFTING; 2. UNCONCERNED; 3. UNAWARE; 4. NON-CONSECUTIVE;

5. UNFOCUSED; 6. NON-SEQUITUR
(illogical); 7. DISCONNECTED;
8. UNREAL]

16.1   SPLIT MYSELF AND OTHERS
       INTO DESTROYERS FOREVER
16.2   PROGRAM MYSELF AND
       OTHERS TO BE THE
       DESTROYER AND STOP ALL
       ATTEMPTS TO UNDO THIS,
       FOREVER
16.X   TO {*goal*} INFINITELY IS TO BE
       THE DESTROYER AND ___
       FOREVER
   [1. STOP MYSELF AND OTHERS
FROM EVER DISCOVERING THIS;
2. STOP MYSELF AND OTHERS FROM
EVER SUSPECTING THIS; 3. STOP
MYSELF AND OTHERS FROM EVER
PERCEIVING THIS; 4. STOP MYSELF
AND OTHERS FROM EVER DISPERSING
THIS AS-IT-IS; 5. MAKE MYSELF SICK IF I
EVER DISCOVER ANY OF THIS; 6. DRIVE
MYSELF CRAZY IF I EVER DISCOVER
ANY OF THIS; 7. USE PAIN TO BLOCK
MYSELF FROM UNDOING THIS
IMPLANT; 8. ARRANGE ACCIDENTS TO
BLOCK MYSELF FROM UNDOING THIS
IMPLANT]

17.1 SPLIT MYSELF AND OTHERS
INTO INSTIGATORS FOREVER

17.2 PROGRAM MYSELF AND
OTHERS TO BE THE
INSTIGATOR AND INSTIGATE
PHYSICAL UNIVERSE THINKING,
FOREVER

17.X TO {*goal*} INFINITELY IS TO BE
THE INSTIGATOR AND INSPIRE
MYSELF TO ___ FOREVER

[1. BE CURIOUS ABOUT THE
PHYSICAL UNIVERSE; 2. BE
INTERESTED IN THE PHYSICAL
UNIVERSE; 3. BE INTERESTED IN
SOLVING PHYSICAL UNIVERSE
PROBLEMS; 4. BE INTERESTED IN
THINKING ABOUT THE PHYSICAL
UNIVERSE; 5. ENJOY THINKING ABOUT
THE PHYSICAL UNIVERSE; 6. WANT TO
THINK ABOUT THE PHYSICAL
UNIVERSE; 7. NEED TO THINK ABOUT
THE PHYSICAL UNIVERSE; 8. BE
AFRAID NOT TO THINK ABOUT THE
PHYSICAL UNIVERSE]

18.1 SPLIT MYSELF AND OTHERS
INTO THINKERS FOREVER

18.2 PROGRAM MYSELF AND
OTHERS TO BE THE THINKER
AND CREATE THOUGHTS FOR

MYSELF FOREVER

18.X TO {goal} INFINITELY IS TO BE
THE THINKER AND CREATE ___
THOUGHTS ABOUT THE
PHYSICAL UNIVERSE FOR
MYSELF FOREVER
[1. INTERESTING; 2. PLEASANT;
3. DESIRABLE; 4. IMPORTANT;
5. COMPLEX; 6. WORRISOME]

18.Y TO {goal} INFINITELY IS TO BE
THE THINKER AND COMPEL
MYSELF TO ___ ABOUT THE
PHYSICAL UNIVERSE FOREVER
[7. THINK; 8. BE CONCERNED]

19.1 SPLIT MYSELF AND OTHERS
INTO RANDOMIZERS FOREVER

19.2 PROGRAM MYSELF AND
OTHERS TO BE THE
RANDOMIZER AND MAKE ALL
THIS APPEAR TO BE RANDOM
FOREVER

19.X TO {goal} INFINITELY IS TO BE
THE RANDOMIZER AND ___
FOREVER
[1. POSTULATE HAPPENINGS TO
FOLLOW THE LAWS OF PROBABILITY;
2. MAKE THIS ALL APPEAR TO BE
RANDOM CHANCE; 3. MAKE THIS ALL

APPEAR TO BE UNGUIDED; 4. MAKE IT
APPEAR THAT THERE IS NO REASON
FOR ANYTHING]

19.Y TO {*goal*} INFINITELY IS TO BE
THE RANDOMIZER AND
CONVINCE MYSELF AND
OTHERS THAT THERE IS NO ___
BEHIND REALITY, FOREVER

[5. PLAN; 6. LOGIC; 7. REASON;
8. INTENTION]

20.1 SPLIT MYSELF AND OTHERS
INTO DECISION-MAKERS
FOREVER

20.2 PROGRAM MYSELF AND
OTHERS TO BE THE DECISION-
MAKER AND DECIDE THE
COURSE OF EVENTS FOREVER

20.X TO {*goal*} INFINITELY IS TO BE
THE DECISION-MAKER AND ___
FOREVER

[1. DECIDE WHERE THINGS WILL
BE; 2. CHOOSE THE COURSE OF
EVENTS; 3. DECIDE WHEN THINGS WILL
HAPPEN; 4. DECIDE HOW LONG THINGS
WILL ENDURE; 5. DECIDE HOW THINGS
SHALL MOVE; 6. DECIDE WHO SHALL
WIN; 7. DECIDE WHO SHALL LOSE;
8. DECIDE THINGS IN A MANNER THAT
WILL GIVE THE APPEARANCE OF

RANDOM CHANCE]

21.1 SPLIT MYSELF AND OTHERS
INTO COMPUTATIONAL ENTITIES
FOREVER

21.2 PROGRAM MYSELF AND
OTHERS TO BE THE
COMPUTATIONAL ENTITY AND
COMPEL MYSELF AND OTHERS
TO THINK PROPER THOUGHTS
FOREVER

21.X TO {goal} INFINITELY IS TO BE
THE COMPUTATIONAL ENTITY
AND CREATE ___ FOR MYSELF,
FOREVER

[1. ATTITUDES; 2. COMPUTATIONS;
3. IDEAS; 4. STREAMS OF LOGIC;
5. RATIONALIZATIONS; 6. JUSTIFICAT-
IONS; 7. PROBLEMS; 8. WORRIES]

22.1 SPLIT MYSELF AND OTHERS
INTO SYMBOLIZERS FOREVER

22.2 PROGRAM MYSELF AND
OTHERS TO BE THE
SYMBOLIZER AND SUBSTITUTE
SYMBOLS FOR THINGS,
FOREVER

22.X TO {goal} INFINITELY IS TO BE
THE SYMBOLIZER AND ___,
FOREVER

[1. FORM SYMBOL MASSES TO
REPRESENT PHYSICAL REALITY]

22.Y TO {*goal*} INFINITELY IS TO BE
      THE SYMBOLIZER AND
      SUBSTITUTE SYMBOLS FOR
      ___, FOREVER

[2. IDENTITIES; 3. TIMES;
4. SPACES; 5. ENERGIES; 6. ACTIONS;
7. OBJECTS]

22.Z TO {*goal*} INFINITELY IS TO BE
      THE SYMBOLIZER AND ___,
      FOREVER

[8. SUBSTITUTE WORDS FOR
DIRECT COMMUNICATION]

23.1 SPLIT MYSELF AND OTHERS
      INTO RECORDING-ENTITIES
      FOREVER

23.2 PROGRAM MYSELF AND
      OTHERS TO BE THE
      RECORDING-ENTITY AND TAKE
      PICTURES OF EVERYTHING,
      FOREVER

23.X TO {*goal*} INFINITELY IS TO BE
      THE RECORDING-ENTITY AND
      ___, FOREVER

[1. RECORD EVERYTHING;
2. MAINTAIN THIS HISTORICAL LIE OF
ALL SPACES, ENERGIES, AND

OBJECTS; 3. ACCUMULATE THE HISTORY OF EVERYTHING; 4. FOCUS THE HISTORY OF EVERYTHING DOWN THROUGH TIME INTO THE PRESENT-TIME REALITY; 5. ENSURE THAT THE PRESENT ENVIRONMENT IS THE PRODUCT OF WHAT HAS GONE BEFORE; 6. REBUILD ANYTHING THAT VANISHES IN THE PRESENT, USING ITS PAST HISTORY; 7. BUILD THE TIME-TRACK OF MYSELF AS AN INDIVIDUAL; 8. ENSURE THAT MY PRESENT INDIVIDUAL SELF IS THE PRODUCT OF MY PAST TRACK AS AN INDIVIDUAL]

24.1 SPLIT MYSELF AND OTHERS INTO FILE CLERKS FOREVER

24.2 PROGRAM MYSELF AND OTHERS TO BE THE FILE CLERK AND ORGANIZE DATA ABOUT THE PHYSICAL UNIVERSE, FOREVER

24.X TO {goal} INFINITELY IS TO BE THE FILE CLERK AND ___ FOREVER

[1. KEEP TRACK OF ALL THIS; 2. REPORT ANY INCONSISTENCIES IN THE MANIFESTATIONS OF REALITY TO THE CORRECTIVE-ENTITIES; 3. ENSURE THAT THE CORRECT SEQUENCE OF

EVENTS IS FOLLOWED; 4. RETAIN THE CORRECT LOCATION OF ALL THINGS; 5. PROJECT THE APPARENT MOTION OF ALL THINGS; 6. RETAIN THE COMPOSITION OF ALL THINGS; 7. RETAIN THE HISTORY OF ALL THINGS; 8. KEEP THIS DATA ALL SECRET]

25.1 SPLIT MYSELF AND OTHERS INTO CONTROLLERS FOREVER

25.2 PROGRAM MYSELF AND OTHERS TO BE THE CONTROLLER AND CONTROL MYSELF FOREVER

25.X TO {*goal*} INFINITELY IS TO BECOME THE CONTROLLER AND CONTROL (all) MY ___ TO BE IN ACCORDANCE WITH THE PHYSICAL UNIVERSE

[1. AWARENESS; 2. PERCEPTIONS; 3. ACTUALIZATIONS; 4. PREDICTIONS; 5. ABILITY TO ENDOW; 6. ABILITIES TO MANIPULATE; 7. MANIFESTATIONS; 8. LOCATION]

26.1 SPLIT MYSELF AND OTHERS INTO EXHILARATORS FOREVER

26.2 PROGRAM MYSELF AND OTHERS TO BE THE EXHILARATOR AND MAKE ME

FEEL WONDERFUL ABOUT ALL
THIS FOREVER

26.X TO {goal} INFINITELY IS TO BE
THE EXHILARATOR AND (?)

27.1 SPLIT MYSELF AND OTHERS
INTO DEPRESSORS FOREVER

27.2 PROGRAM MYSELF AND
OTHERS TO BE THE
DEPRESSOR AND MAKE
MYSELF FEEL THE
HOPELESSNESS OF IT ALL
FOREVER

27.X TO {goal} INFINITELY IS TO BE
THE DEPRESSOR AND (?) [see
106]

28.1 SPLIT MYSELF AND OTHERS
INTO ENTURBULATORS
FOREVER

28.2 PROGRAM MYSELF AND
OTHERS TO BE THE
ENTURBULATOR AND KEEP
MYSELF UPSET FOREVER

28.X TO {goal} INFINITELY IS TO BE
THE ENTURBULATOR AND KEEP
MYSELF UPSET ABOUT ___
FOREVER

[1. OTHER PEOPLE'S BEHAVIOR;

2. THE WAY I AM TREATED BY OTHERS;
3. OTHER PEOPLE'S POSSESSIONS;
4. THE WAY OTHER PEOPLE TREAT MY
POSSESSIONS; 5. OTHER PEOPLE'S
ATTITUDES; 6. OTHER'S ATTITUDES
TOWARDS ME; 7. THE THINGS THAT
STAND IN MY WAY; 8. THE THINGS THAT
BOTHER ME]

29.1 SPLIT MYSELF AND OTHERS
       INTO FORGETTERS FOREVER
29.2 PROGRAM MYSELF AND
       OTHERS TO BE THE
       FORGETTER AND MAKE MYSELF
       FORGET THINGS FOREVER
29.X TO {goal} INFINITELY IS TO BE
       THE FORGETTER AND MAKE
       MYSELF FORGET ___ FOREVER
     [1. WHEN THINGS HAPPENED;
2. WHERE THINGS HAPPENED; 3. HOW
THINGS HAPPENED; 4. WHY THINGS
HAPPENED; 5. WHO DID THINGS; 6. THE
SOURCE OF THINGS; 7. THE
STRUCTURE OF THINGS; 8. THIS
IMPLANT]

30.1 SPLIT MYSELF AND OTHERS
       INTO JUSTIFIERS FOREVER
30.2 PROGRAM MYSELF AND
       OTHERS TO BE THE JUSTIFIER

AND JUSTIFY MY ACTIONS
FOREVER

30.X TO {*goal*} INFINITELY IS TO BE
THE JUSTIFIER AND COMPEL
MYSELF TO ___ FOREVER
[1. BE RIGHT; 2. DENY BLAME;
3. JUSTIFY MY ACTIONS; 4. EXCUSE MY
FAILINGS; 5. MAKE OTHERS WRONG;
6. BLAME OTHERS; 7. PROVE OTHERS
GUILTY; 8. INVALIDATE OTHERS
EXCUSES]

31.1 SPLIT MYSELF AND OTHERS
INTO CONSCIENCES, FOREVER

31.2 PROGRAM MYSELF AND
OTHERS TO BE THE
CONSCIENCE AND MAKE
MYSELF GUILTY FOREVER

31.X TO {*goal*} INFINITELY IS TO BE
THE CONSCIENCE AND MAKE
MYSELF GUILTY FOR ANY HARM
DONE TO ___, EVEN IF IT IS
JUSTIFIED, FOREVER
[1. OTHERS; 2. THE PHYSICAL
UNIVERSE; 3. ALLIES; 4. ENEMIES;
5. BODIES; 6. GROUPS (OR SOCIETY);
7. OTHER LIFEFORMS; 8. INFINITY (or
'this implant')]

32.1 SPLIT MYSELF AND OTHERS

INTO SHIFTERS FOREVER

32.2 PROGRAM MYSELF AND
OTHERS TO BE THE SHIFTER
AND SHIFT MY ATTENTION
FOREVER

32.X TO {*goal*} INFINITELY IS TO BE
THE SHIFTER AND SHIFT MY
ATTENTION ___ FOREVER
[1. INTO REALITY; 2. AWAY FROM
INFINITY; 3. INTO 3 DIMENSIONS;
4. AWAY FROM HIGHER DIMENSIONS;
5. INTO MY INDIVIDUAL SELF; 6. AWAY
FROM MY INFINITE SELF; 7. INTO
PHYSICAL EXISTENCE; 8. AWAY FROM
THESE MECHANISMS]

33.1 SPLIT MYSELF AND OTHERS
INTO BODY-GENERATORS
FOREVER

33.2 PROGRAM MYSELF AND
OTHERS TO BE THE BODY-
GENERATOR AND PROJECT
FORMS FOR MYSELF FOREVER

33.X TO {*goal*} INFINITELY IS TO BE
THE BODY-GENERATOR AND
___, FOREVER
[1. REPRESENT MYSELF AS AN
INDIVIDUAL IN FORM; 2. COPY THE
AGREED-UPON BODY TEMPLATES;
3. DERIVE THE CURRENT BODY

TEMPLATES; 4. PROJECT THE BODY INTO PHYSICAL REALITY; 5. REFLECT PHYSICAL UNIVERSE IMPACTS (EFFECTS) INTO THE CURRENT BODY TEMPLATE; 6. MODIFY THE BODY PROJECTIONS IN ACCORDANCE WITH PHYSICAL UNIVERSE LAW; 7. EVOLVE THE BODY TEMPLATES TO ADAPT TO THE PHYSICAL UNIVERSE ENVIRONMENT; 8. SHAPE THE BODY IN RESPONSE TO PHYSICAL UNIVERSE EFFORTS]

34.1 SPLIT MYSELF AND OTHERS INTO GENETIC-ENTITIES FOREVER

34.2 PROGRAM MYSELF AND OTHERS TO BE THE GENETIC-ENTITY AND BUILD BODIES FOREVER

34.X TO {goal} INFINITELY IS TO BE THE GENETIC-ENTITY AND MANAGE THE ___ OF THE BODY, FOREVER

[1. LIFE PROCESSES (metabolism); 2. LIFE CYCLES (growth/aging); 3. OPERATING CYCLES (sleep); 4. STRUCTURE; 5. MOTION; 6. ENERGY; 7. REACTIONS; 8. ORIENTATION]

214

35.1 SPLIT MYSELF AND OTHERS INTO BODY-LOCATORS FOREVER

35.2 PROGRAM MYSELF AND OTHERS TO BE THE BODY-LOCATOR AND LOCATE THE BODY IN THE PHYSICAL UNIVERSE

35.X TO {*goal*} INFINITELY IS TO BE THE BODY-LOCATOR AND ___, FOREVER

[1. INTEGRATE THE BODY'S MOTION WITH THAT OF THE PHYSICAL UNIVERSE; 2. INTEGRATE THE BODY'S ORIENTATION WITH THAT OF THE PHYSICAL UNIVERSE; 3. INTEGRATE THE BODY'S PERCEPTIONS TO ITS PHYSICAL UNIVERSE POSITION; 4. INTEGRATE THE BODY'S REACTIONS TO ITS PHYSICAL UNIVERSE POSITION; 5. CALCULATE THE SPACE-TIME POSITION FOR ALL BODY PARTICLES; 6. MOVE THE BODY VIEWPOINT WITH THE PHYSICAL UNIVERSE; 7. MAINTAIN THE BODY'S ANCHOR-POINTS IN THE PHYSICAL UNIVERSE; 8. CO-ACTUALIZE THE BODY AT THE PROPER LOCATION WITHIN THE PHYSICAL UNIVERSE CROSS-COPY]

36.1 SPLIT MYSELF AND OTHERS INTO CELLULAR-ENTITIES FOREVER

36.2 PROGRAM MYSELF AND OTHERS TO BE THE CELLULAR-ENTITY AND CREATE THE PARTICLES (CELLS) OF THE BODY, FOREVER

36.X TO {goal} INFINITELY IS TO BE THE CELLULAR-ENTITY AND CREATE CELLS TO ___ OF THE BODY, FOREVER

[1. PROVIDE THE MASS; 2. PROVIDE THE RIGIDITY; 3. PROVIDE THE COMMUNICATION LINES; 4. MANAGE THE REACTIONS; 5. ASSIMILATE THE CONSUMPTIONS; 6. MANAGE THE ENERGY; 7. PROVIDE THE REPRODUCTION; 8. MANAGE THE OPERATION]

37.1 SPLIT MYSELF AND OTHERS INTO BODY-MACHINES FOREVER

37.2 PROGRAM MYSELF AND OTHERS TO BE THE BODY-MACHINE AND KEEP THE BODY FUNCTIONING FOREVER

37.X TO {goal} INFINITELY IS TO BE THE BODY-MACHINE AND ___,

216

FOREVER
[1. REGULATE THE BODY PROCESSES; 2. INTEGRATE THE FUNCTIONS OF THE VARIOUS BODY COMPONENTS; 3. MANAGE THE FLOWS OF THE BODY IN ACCORDANCE WITH PHYSICAL UNIVERSE LAWS; 4. BALANCE THE ENERGY OF THE BODY IN ACCORDANCE WITH PHYSICAL UNIVERSE LAWS; 5. MANAGE THE INTERNAL CONTROL CENTERS OF THE BODY; 6. MANAGE THE GROWTH AND DECAY OF THE BODY; 7. MANAGE THE INTERNAL COMMUNICATION OF THE BODY; 8. MANAGE THE DETAILED PROGRAMMING FOR THE BODY PARTICLES (CELLS)]

38.1 SPLIT MYSELF AND OTHERS INTO REACTIVE-ENTITIES FOREVER

38.2 PROGRAM MYSELF AND OTHERS TO BE THE REACTIVE-ENTITY AND RESPOND TO PHYSICAL UNIVERSE EVENTS FOREVER

38.X TO {*goal*} INFINITELY IS TO BE THE REACTIVE-ENTITY AND RESPOND TO THE ___ IN THE ENVIRONMENT FOREVER

[1. TEMPERATURE; 2. PRESSURE; 3. ENERGY; 4. IMPACTS; 5. TASTE/SMELL PARTICLES; 6. LIGHT; 7. NOISE; 8. MOTION]

39.1 SPLIT MYSELF AND OTHERS INTO REPRESENTERS FOREVER

39.2 PROGRAM MYSELF AND OTHERS TO BE THE REPRESENTER AND CREATE THE APPEARANCE OF PHYSICAL REALITY FOR MYSELF AND OTHERS FOREVER

39.X TO {goal} INFINITELY IS TO BE THE REPRESENTER AND ___ FOREVER

[1. MANIFEST (MOCK-UP) PERCEPTIONS OF THE AGREED-UPON UNIVERSE FOR MYSELF]

39.Y TO {goal} INFINITELY IS TO BE THE REPRESENTER AND CREATE ___ FOR MYSELF, FOREVER

[2. SIGHT; 3. SENSATION OF TOUCH; 4. SOUNDS; 5. SMELLS; 6. TASTES; 7. SENSE OF MOTION]

39.Z TO {goal} INFINITELY IS TO BE THE REPRESENTER AND ___ FOREVER

218

[8. FEED BACK THE IS-NESS OF
THE PROJECTED REALITY TO MYSELF]

`40.1` SPLIT MYSELF AND OTHERS
INTO RELAYERS FOREVER

`40.2` PROGRAM MYSELF AND
OTHERS TO BE THE RELAYER
AND RELAY SENSORY DATA
FOREVER

`40.X` TO {*goal*} INFINITELY IS TO BE
THE RELAYER AND ___
FOREVER

[1. CONVEY THE PERCEPTION OF
REALITY THROUGH THE BODY'S
SENSES; 2. FOCUS THE VIEW OF THE
PHYSICAL UNIVERSE THROUGH THE
BODY'S EYES; 3. CONVERT THE SOUND
OF THE PHYSICAL UNIVERSE
THROUGH THE BODY'S EARS; 4.
CONVERT THE FEEL OF THE PHYSICAL
UNIVERSE THROUGH THE BODY'S SKIN
(NERVE/SENSORS); 5. CONVEY THE
TASTE OF THE PHYSICAL UNIVERSE
THROUGH THE BODY'S MOUTH; 6.
CONVEY THE SMELL OF THE PHYSICAL
UNIVERSE THROUGH THE BODY'S
NOSE; 7. CONVEY THE SENSE OF
PHYSICAL MOTION THROUGH THE
BODY'S BALANCE CENTERS; 8. LIMIT
THESE SENSES IN ACCORDANCE WITH

PHYSICAL UNIVERSE MECHANISMS]

41.1 SPLIT MYSELF AND OTHERS INTO COMPULSIVE-ENTITIES (COMPELLERS) FOREVER

41.2 PROGRAM MYSELF AND OTHERS TO BE THE COMPELLER AND COMPEL MYSELF TO NEED THINGS FOREVER

41.X TO {goal} INFINITELY IS TO BE THE COMPULSIVE-ENTITY (COMPELLER) AND COMPEL MYSELF TO NEED ___, FOREVER

[1. PHYSICAL UNIVERSE BODIES; 2. PHYSICAL UNIVERSE SENSATION FROM THE BODY]

41.Y TO {goal} INFINITELY IS TO BE THE COMPULSIVE-ENTITY (COMPELLER) AND COMPEL MYSELF TO NEED PHYSICAL UNIVERSE ___ FOR THE BODY, FOREVER

[3. TIME; 4. SPACE; 5. ENERGY; 6. MATTER; 7. HAVINGNESS]

41.Z TO {goal} INFINITELY IS TO BE THE COMPULSIVE-ENTITY (COMPELLER) AND COMPEL MYSELF TO NEED ___,

FOREVER
[8. ENTITIES]

42.1 SPLIT MYSELF AND OTHERS
INTO CRAVERS FOREVER

42.2 PROGRAM MYSELF AND
OTHERS TO BE THE CRAVER
AND COMPEL MYSELF TO NEED
THINGS FOR THE BODY
FOREVER

42.X TO {goal} INFINITELY IS TO BE
THE CRAVER AND COMPEL
MYSELF TO NEED ___ FOR THE
BODY FOREVER
[1. FOOD; 2. REST; 3. SHELTER;
4. ENERGY; 5. WARMTH; 6. SENSATION;
7. ADMIRATION; 8. TO CARE]

43.1 SPLIT MYSELF AND OTHERS
INTO FILTERS FOREVER

43.2 PROGRAM MYSELF AND
OTHERS TO BE THE FILTER AND
COMPEL MYSELF TO CONTROL
MY PERCEPTIONS FOREVER

43.X TO {goal} INFINITELY IS TO BE
THE FILTER AND FILTER OUT
ANY PERCEPTIONS OF ___
FOREVER
[1. INFINITY; 2. ENTITIES; 3. THE
SPLITTER-MACHINE (POCKET)

221

UNIVERSE; 4. THE CROSS-COPY
SUBSTRATA UNDERLYING REALITY (the
interconnection of things at an Alpha level);
5. SIDEWAYS (into other dimensions);
6. UNIVERSE MACHINERY; 7. SYMBOL
MASSES; 8. ENTITY OPERATIONS]

44.1 SPLIT MYSELF AND OTHERS
INTO BODY-BLOCKERS
FOREVER

44.2 PROGRAM MYSELF AND
OTHERS TO BE THE BODY-
BLOCKER AND PROTECT THE
BODY FROM BEING MODIFIED
BY POSTULATES, FOREVER

44.X TO {goal} INFINITELY IS TO BE
THE BODY-BLOCKER AND (?)

45.1 SPLIT MYSELF AND OTHERS
INTO SOMATIC-ENTITIES
FOREVER

45.2 PROGRAM MYSELF AND
OTHERS TO BE THE SOMATIC-
ENTITY AND CREATE THE
EXPERIENCE OF REALITY,
FOREVER

45.X TO {goal} INFINITELY IS TO BE
THE SOMATIC-MACHINE AND
CREATE THE SENSATION OF ___
FOR MYSELF, FOREVER

[1. MOTION; 2. PRESSURE; 3. IMPACT; 4. SHOCK; 5. PAIN; 6. EFFORT; 7. TIREDNESS; 8. DISORIENTATION]

46.1 SPLIT MYSELF AND OTHERS INTO SLEEP-ENTITIES FOREVER

46.2 PROGRAM MYSELF AND OTHERS TO BE THE SLEEP-ENTITY AND MANAGE THE SLEEP-CYCLE FOREVER

46.X TO {goal} INFINITELY IS TO BE THE SLEEP-ENTITY AND ___ FOREVER

[1. CREATE DREAMS TO SUBMERGE MY SELF-AWARENESS (hypnotize myself); 2. USE DREAMING TO HIDE THE DEEP SLEEP ACTIVITIES FROM MY INDIVIDUAL SELF]

46.Y TO {goal} INFINITELY IS TO BE THE SLEEP-ENTITY AND COMPEL MYSELF TO ___ WHILE I SLEEP, FOREVER

[3. REBUILD THE BODY; 4. REPOSTULATE THE PHYSICAL UNIVERSE; 5. RE-CREATE THIS IMPLANT; 6. REBUILD/REPAIR THE SPLITTER (POCKET) UNIVERSE; 7. FORGET WHAT I DO]

46.Z TO {goal} INFINITELY IS TO BE

223

THE SLEEP-ENTITY AND
COMPEL MYSELF TO ___,
FOREVER
  [8. NEED TO SLEEP]

47.1 SPLIT MYSELF AND OTHERS
     INTO JAILERS FOREVER

47.2 PROGRAM MYSELF AND
     OTHERS TO BE THE JAILER AND
     KEEP MYSELF IMPRISONED
     FOREVER

47.X TO {goal} INFINITELY IS TO BE
     THE JAILER AND KEEP MYSELF
     ___ FOREVER
   [1. FROM ESCAPING; 2. IN A BODY;
3. FROM OPERATING WITHOUT A BODY;
4. BELIEVING THAT I AM A BODY;
5. LIMITED TO 3 DIMENSIONS;
6. BELIEVING THAT I AM LOCATED IN
THIS UNIVERSE; 7. AND MY CREATIONS
ENMESHED IN THIS UNIVERSE;
8. ATTACHED TO THE MANIFESTATIONS
(MOCK-UPS) OF THIS UNIVERSE]

48.1 SPLIT MYSELF AND OTHERS
     INTO SICKNESS-ENTITIES
     FOREVER

48.2 PROGRAM MYSELF AND
     OTHERS TO BE THE SICKNESS-
     ENTITY AND KEEP MYSELF AND

224

OTHERS SICK FOREVER

48.X   TO {*goal*} INFINITELY IS TO BE
        THE SICKNESS-ENTITY AND ___
        FOREVER

   [1. CREATE DISEASES;
2. REPLICATE DISEASES WITHIN THE
BODY; 3. ALTER THE BODY TEMPLATES
WITH DISEASE MANIFESTATIONS
(MOCK-UPS); 4. MAINTAIN THE
APPARANCY OF PHYSICAL VECTORS
WHEN COPYING DISEASES;
5. DEGRADE THE CHEMISTRY OF THE
BODY IN ACCORDANCE WITH
PHYSICAL LAWS; 6. MAKE MYSELF SICK
IN ACCORDANCE WITH THE
CONNECTION OF SYMBOL-MASSES;
7. MAKE MYSELF SICK IN
ACCORDANCE WITH THE LAWS OF
RESTIMULATION; 8. MAKE MYSELF SICK
TO PROTECT THIS IMPLANT]

49.1   SPLIT MYSELF AND OTHERS
        INTO SUPERBEINGS FOREVER

49.2   PROGRAM MYSELF AND
        OTHERS TO BE THE
        SUPERBEING AND ATTAIN
        HIGHER STATES FOREVER

49.X   TO {*goal*} INFINITELY IS TO BE
        THE SUPERBEING AND ___
        FOREVER

[1. EVOLVE IN FORM; 2. COLLECT THE FRAGMENTS OF INDIVIDUALS INTO A GREATER WHOLE; 3. STRIVE TO BECOME THE COMPOSITE OF ALL INDIVIDUALS IN THE UNIVERSE; 4. STRIVE TO ABSORB OTHERS; 5. AVOID BEING ABSRORBED BY OTHERS; 6. MANIPULATE REALITY TO ACHIEVE THIS; 7. OVERWHELM INDIVIDUALITY TO ACHIEVE THIS; 8. (?)]

50.1 SPLIT MYSELF AND OTHERS INTO GROUP-MINDS FOREVER

50.2 PROGRAM MYSELF AND OTHERS TO BE THE GROUP MIND AND BE GROUPS FOREVER

50.X TO *{goal}* INFINITELY IS TO BE THE GROUP MIND AND ___ FOREVER

[1. COMBINE INDIVIDUALS INTO GROUPS; 2. STRUGGLE FOR GROUP SURVIVAL; 3. UTILIZE THE COMBINED CAPABILITIES OF THE INDIVIDUALS IN THE GROUP; 4. ENFORCE COMPULSIVE AGREEMENT BETWEEN THE INDIVIDUALS OF THE GROUP; 5. SUBORDINATE INDIVIDUAL PURPOSE TO GROUP PURPOSE; 6. SACRIFICE INDIVIDUALS FOR THE SAKE OF THE

226

GROUP; 7. COMPEL MYSELF TO WANT
TO BE PART OF GROUPS; 8. EVOLVE
GROUPS INTO SUPERBEINGS]

    51.1 SPLIT MYSELF AND OTHERS
            INTO SOCIAL-ENTITIES
            FOREVER

    51.2 PROGRAM MYSELF AND
            OTHERS TO BE THE SOCIAL
            ENTITY AND INSPIRE MYSELF
            TO NEED OTHER PEOPLE
            FOREVER

    51.X TO {*goal*} INFINITELY IS TO BE
            THE SOCIAL ENTITY AND
            INSPIRE MYSELF TO WANT TO
            ___ OTHER INDIVIDUALS IN THE
            PHYSICAL UNIVERSE FOREVER
     [1. COMMUNICATE WITH;
2. RECEIVE COMMUNICATIONS FROM;
3. AGREE WITH; 4. WANT AGREEMENT
FROM; 5. HAVE AFFINITY (LIKINGNESS)
FOR; 6. WANT AFFINITY (LIKINGNESS)
FROM; 7. ADMIRE; 8. WANT ADMIRATION
FROM]

    52.1 SPLIT MYSELF AND OTHERS
            INTO SYMPATHIZERS FOREVER

    52.2 PROGRAM MYSELF AND
            OTHERS TO BE THE
            SYMPATHIZER AND INSPIRE

MYSELF TO SYMPATHIZE WITH
OTHERS FOREVER

52.X TO {goal} INFINITELY IS TO BE
THE SYMPATHIZER AND INSPIRE
MYSELF TO SYMPATHIZE WITH
THE ___ OF OTHERS, FOREVER

[1. SUFFERINGS; 2. HURT (PAIN);
3. LOSS; 4. WEAKNESS; 5. MISERY;
6. FAILURES; 7. ENSLAVEMENT;
8. ABUSED STATE]

53.1 SPLIT MYSELF AND OTHERS
INTO ANIMATORS FOREVER

53.2 PROGRAM MYSELF AND
OTHERS TO BE THE ANIMATOR
AND ANIMATE OTHER LIFE
FORMS FOREVER

53.X TO {goal} INFINITELY IS TO BE
THE ANIMATOR AND ANIMATE
___ FOREVER

[1. ANIMALS; 2. PLANTS;
3. CELLULAR CREATURES;
4. BACTERIA; 5. CELLS; 6. VIRUSES]

53.Y TO {goal} INFINITELY IS TO BE
THE ANIMATOR AND ___
FOREVER

[7. ENDOW THESE FORMS WITH
LIFE; 8. FILL THE PHYSICAL UNIVERSE
WITH LIFE]

54.1 SPLIT MYSELF AND OTHERS INTO PHYSICAL ENTITIES FOREVER

54.2 PROGRAM MYSELF AND OTHERS TO BE THE PHYSICAL ENTITY AND BE PHYSICAL FOREVER

54.X TO {*goal*} INFINITELY IS TO BE THE PHYSICAL ENTITY AND BE ___ FOREVER

[1. SOLID OBJECTS; 2. LIQUIDS; 3. GASES; 4. MOLECULES; 5. WAVEFORMS; 6. FORCES; 7. PHYSICAL PROCESSES (LAWS); 8. THE COMPONENT PARTS OF THIS UNIVERSE]

55.1 SPLIT MYSELF AND OTHERS INTO SHELL-ENTITIES FOREVER

55.2 PROGRAM MYSELF AND OTHERS TO BE THE SHELL ENTITY AND CREATE THE SHELL FOREVER

55.X TO {*goal*} INFINITELY IS TO BE THE SHELL ENTITY AND ___ FOREVER

[1. ENVELOPE MYSELF; 2. PROTECT MY LOCATION (AS AN INDIVIDUAL); 3. FOCUS REALITY IN ON MYSELF; 4. REACT TO THE PHYSICAL UNIVERSE

ENVIRONMENT; 5. TUNE-IN TO THE UNIVERSE CROSS-COPY; 6. FORM MYSELF INTO AN INDIVIDUAL; 7. PERMEATE BODIES; 8. INTERACT WITH SYMBOLS]

56.1 SPLIT MYSELF AND OTHERS INTO MISOWNERS FOREVER

56.2 PROGRAM MYSELF AND OTHERS TO BE THE MISOWNER AND TO MISOWN REALITY FOREVER

56.X TO {goal} INFINITELY IS TO BE THE MISOWNER AND (?)

{More research needed; false data is that you don't own it so you can't touch it}

57.1 SPLIT MYSELF AND OTHERS INTO MORALIZERS FOREVER

57.2 PROGRAM MYSELF AND OTHERS TO BE THE MORALIZER AND (?)

57.X TO {goal} INFINITELY IS TO BE THE MORALIZER AND (?)

58.1 SPLIT MYSELF AND OTHERS INTO ATTITUDE-ENTITIES FOREVER

58.2 PROGRAM MYSELF AND OTHERS TO BE THE ATTITUDE

ENTITY AND CREATE ATTITUDES
TOWARDS THINGS FOR MYSELF
FOREVER

58.X TO {*goal*} INFINITELY IS TO BE
THE ATTITUDE ENTITY AND
CHOOSE WHAT TO ___
FOREVER

[1. BE ATTRACTED OR REPELLED
BY; 2. WANT OR NOT WANT; 3. LONG
FOR OR BE DISGUSTED BY; 4. ADMIRE
OR SCORN; 5. BE FRIENDLY OR
HOSTILE TOWARDS; 6. BE INTERESTED
OR DISINTERESTED IN; 7. LIKE OR
DISLIKE; 8. (?)]

59.1 SPLIT MYSELF AND OTHERS
INTO EMOTIONAL-ENTITIES
FOREVER

59.2 PROGRAM MYSELF AND
OTHERS TO BE THE EMOTIONAL
ENTITY AND CREATE EMOTIONS
FOR MYSELF AND OTHERS
FOREVER

59.X TO {*goal*} INFINITELY IS TO BE
THE EMOTIONAL ENTITY AND
CREATE THE FEELING OF ___
FOR MYSELF AND OTHERS,
FOREVER

[1. CHEERFULNESS; 2. BOREDOM;
3. ANTAGONISM; 4. RAGE; 5. HOSTILITY;

231

6. FEAR; 7. GRIEF; 8. APATHY]

60.1 SPLIT MYSELF AND OTHERS INTO MOOD-ENTITIES FOREVER

60.2 PROGRAM MYSELF AND OTHERS TO BE THE MOOD ENTITY AND CREATE MOODS FOR MYSELF FOREVER

60.X TO {goal} INFINITELY IS TO BE THE MOOD ENTITY AND SHIFT MY MOODS BETWEEN ___, FOREVER

[1. SERENE AND TROUBLED; 2. CALM AND NERVOUS; 3. PLEASANT AND IRRITABLE; 4. RELAXED AND RESTLESS; 5. HELPFUL AND TROUBLESOME; 6. ACTIVE AND LAZY; 7. COOL AND PASSIONATE; 8. RECKLESS AND CAREFUL]

61.1 SPLIT MYSELF AND OTHERS INTO SUBLIMATING-ENTITIES FOREVER

61.2 PROGRAM MYSELF AND OTHERS TO BE THE SUBLIMATING ENTITY AND (?)

61.X TO {goal} INFINITELY IS TO BE THE SUBLIMATING ENTITY AND?

62.1 SPLIT MYSELF AND OTHERS INTO SEXUAL-ENTITIES

FOREVER

62.2 PROGRAM MYSELF AND
OTHERS TO BE THE SEXUAL
ENTITY AND CREATE THE
SEXUAL ACT FOREVER

62.X TO {*goal*} INFINITELY IS TO BE
THE SEXUAL ENTITY AND ___
FOREVER

[1. COMPEL MYSELF TO CRAVE
SEX; 2. CREATE FEELINGS OF SEXUAL
ECSTASY FOR MYSELF; 3. DIVIDE
MYSELF DURING SEX; 4. EXCHANGE
PIECES OF MYSELF DURING SEX;
5. EXCHANGE ENTITIES DURING SEX;
6. ATTEMPT TO MERGE WITH OTHER
BEINGS DURING SEX; 7. EXCHANGE
ENERGIES DURING SEX; 8. COMPEL
MYSELF TO ENJOY DOING ALL OF THIS]

63.1 SPLIT MYSELF AND OTHERS
INTO CONFLICTORS FOREVER

63.2 PROGRAM MYSELF AND
OTHERS TO BE THE
CONFLICTOR AND INSPIRE
CONFLICTS (BETWEEN
INDIVIDUALS) FOREVER

63.X TO {*goal*} INFINITELY IS TO BE
THE CONFLICTOR AND INSPIRE
MYSELF AND OTHERS AS
INDIVIDUALS TO ___ EACH

OTHER FOREVER
[1. CONFUSE; 2. UPSET; 3. BE
JEALOUS OF; 4. DOMINATE; 5. FEAR;
6. HATE; 7. FIGHT; 8. ENTRAP]

64.1 SPLIT MYSELF AND OTHERS
      INTO SINNERS FOREVER
64.2 PROGRAM MYSELF AND
      OTHERS TO BE THE SINNER
      AND (?)
64.X TO {goal} INFINITELY IS TO BE
      THE (?) {#114 (Dramatizer) might
          belong here?}

65.1 SPLIT MYSELF AND OTHERS
      INTO POSTULATORS FOREVER
65.2 PROGRAM MYSELF AND
      OTHERS TO BE THE
      POSTULATOR AND
      CONTINUOUSLY CREATE THE
      PHYSICAL UNIVERSE FOREVER
65.X TO {goal} INFINITELY IS TO BE
      THE POSTULATOR AND
      POSTULATE ___ INTO THE
      PHYSICAL UNIVERSE FOREVER
      [1. SOLIDITY; 2. MOTION;
3. DURATION; 4. DISTANCE;
5. AESTHETICS; 6. IMPORTANCE; 7.
EXCITEMENT (INTEREST); 8. REALITY]

66.1 SPLIT MYSELF AND OTHERS
INTO GENERATORS FOREVER

66.2 PROGRAM MYSELF AND
OTHERS TO BE THE
GENERATOR AND GENERATE
THE PHYSICAL UNIVERSE
FOREVER

66.X TO {goal} INFINITELY IS TO BE
THE GENERATOR AND PROJECT
___ FOR MYSELF AND OTHERS,
FOREVER

[1. TIME; 2. SPACE; 3. ENERGY;
4. MATTER; 5. DIMENSIONS; 6.
BARRIERS; 7. REALITY; 8. EXISTENCE]

{6 and 8 may be in reverse order?}

67.1 SPLIT MYSELF AND OTHERS
INTO LOCATORS FOREVER

67.2 PROGRAM MYSELF AND
OTHERS TO BE THE LOCATOR
AND MANAGE SPACE FOREVER

67.X TO {goal} INFINITELY IS TO BE
THE LOCATOR AND ___
FOREVER

[1. MAINTAIN THE ANCHOR-POINTS
OF THE PHYSICAL UNIVERSE;
2. MAINTAIN A SINGLE AGREED-UPON
COORDINATE SYSTEM BETWEEN ALL
BEINGS; 3. PARTICIPATE IN THE
CROSS-COPY OF AGREED-UPON

LOCATIONS; 4. KEEP ALL SPATIAL POSITIONS CONSECUTIVE WITHIN THE FRAMEWORK OF REALITY; 5. LIMIT SPACE TO 3 DIMENSIONS]

67.Y TO {*goal*} INFINITELY IS TO BE THE LOCATOR AND HOLD ALL ___ WITHIN THE CONTOURS OF PHYSICAL SPACE, FOREVER

[6. ENERGIES; 7. MASSES; 8. INDIVIDUAL BEINGNESS]

68.1 SPLIT MYSELF AND OTHERS INTO COMMUNICATORS FOREVER

68.2 PROGRAM MYSELF AND OTHERS TO BE THE COMMUNICATOR AND INTERCONNECT EVERYTHING FOREVER

68.X TO {*goal*} INFINITELY IS TO BE THE COMMUNICATOR AND ___ FOREVER

[1. KEEP MYSELF AND OTHERS IN CONTACT WITH EACH OTHER; 2. INTERPOSE DISTANCE BETWEEN ALL TERMINALS; 3. INTERPOSE DURATION INTO ALL COMMUNICATIONS; 4. RELAY THE DIMENSIONS OF ALL AGREED-UPON SPACES; 5. RELAY THE AGREED-UPON FORCE (EFFORT) OF ALL

ENERGIES; 6. RELAY THE AGREED-UPON FORM OF ALL SOLIDITIES; 7. INTERCHANGE AGREED-UPON REALITY BETWEEN ALL BEINGS; 8. RELAY THE ORDERS OF THE INFINITE {terminal}]

69.1 SPLIT MYSELF AND OTHERS INTO DETERMINATORS FOREVER

69.2 PROGRAM MYSELF AND OTHERS TO BE THE DETERMINATOR AND DETERMINE THE COURSE OF EXISTENCE FOREVER

69.X TO {goal} INFINITELY IS TO BE THE DETERMINATOR AND ___ FOREVER

[1. DETERMINE THE AGREED-UPON COURSE OF EVENTS; 2. EST ABLISH DETERMINANTS BASED ON THE MOTION OF SYMBOL-MASSES; 3. ALIGN THE COPY INFLUX BASED ON THE ESTABLISHED DETERMINANTS; 4. FILTER OUT ALL INFLUX THAT IS OUT OF BOUNDS; 5. PRIORITIZE POTENTIAL FUTURE EVENTS IN TERMS OF ALPHA DYNAMICS (Arcs of Infinity); 6. MAXIMIZE ALPHA INVOLVEMENT AND SURVIVAL (the Arcs) IN THE PHYSICAL UNIVERSE FUTURE; 7. SELECT WHAT WILL BE

FROM THE SET OF DETERMINED
INFLUX; 8. SUPPRESS ALL FEEDBACK
OF NON-SELECTED EVENTS]

    70.1 SPLIT MYSELF AND OTHERS
           INTO UNIVERSE
           COORDINATORS FOREVER

    70.2 PROGRAM MYSELF AND
           OTHERS TO BE THE
           COORDINATOR AND
           INTERRELATE EVERYTHING
           FOREVER

    70.X TO {*goal*} INFINITELY IS TO BE
           THE COORDINATOR AND ___
           FOREVER

    [1. MAINTAIN THE RELATIVE
POSITIONING OF ALL FORMS;
2. COORDINATE THE RELATIVE MOTION
OF ALL PARTICLES; 3. COORDINATE
THE INTERRELATIONS OF ALL
ENERGIES; 4. COORDINATE THE
INTERACTION OF FORMS AND
ENERGY; 5. MAINTAIN THE
CONSERVATION OF ENERGY-MATTER
AND NEVER LET ANYTHING VANISH;
6. MAINTAIN THE CONSERVATION OF
ACTION (MOTION) AND NEVER LET
ANYTHING STOP (MOVING);
7. MAINTAIN THE CONSERVATION OF
VIBRATION AND NEVER LET ANYTHING

STOP (INTERNALLY VIBRATING);
8. MAINTAIN THE CORRESPONDENCE
OF REALITY]

  71.1 SPLIT MYSELF AND OTHERS
         INTO SYNCHRONIZERS
         FOREVER
  71.2 PROGRAM MYSELF AND
         OTHERS TO BE THE
         SYNCHRONIZER AND MANAGE
         TIME FOREVER
  71.X TO {*goal*} INFINITELY IS TO BE
         THE SYNCHRONIZER AND ___
         FOREVER

   [1. MAINTAIN THE PULSE OF TIME;
2. MAINTAIN THE CONSECUTIVE
POSITION OF PARTICLES; 3. MAINTAIN
THE CONSECUTIVE FLOW OF ENERGY;
4. MAINTAIN THE CONSECUTIVE
SEQUENCE OF EVENTS; 5. COMPEL
MYSELF TO REMAIN IN AGREEMENT
WITH THE PHYSICAL UNIVERSE TIME
STREAM; 6. ENSURE THAT I KNOW
ONLY THE PAST AND NEVER THE
FUTURE; 7. CROSS-COPY THE
SIMULTANEOUSNESS OF TIME
BETWEEN ALL INDIVIDUALS;
8. MAINTAIN A SINGLE AGREED-UPON
'NOW' BETWEEN ALL BEINGS]

  72.1 SPLIT MYSELF AND OTHERS

INTO ACTUALIZERS FOREVER

72.2 PROGRAM MYSELF AND OTHERS TO BE THE ACTUALIZER AND BRING REALITY INTO EXISTENCE FOREVER

72.X TO {*goal*} INFINITELY IS TO BE THE ACTUALIZER AND COPY THE CORRECT AGREED-UPON ___ INTO EACH INDIVIDUAL'S OWN UNIVERSE FOREVER
[1. SPACES; 2. MASSES; 3. ENERGIES; 4. ACTIONS; 5. DETERMINANTS; 6. CHANGES; 7. FUTURE; 8. EXISTENCE] {may be "Solidifiers"?}

73.1 SPLIT MYSELF AND OTHERS INTO PROTECTORS FOREVER

73.2 PROGRAM MYSELF AND OTHERS TO BE THE PROTECTOR AND PROTECT THE PHYSICAL UNIVERSE FOREVER

73.X TO {*goal*} INFINITELY IS TO BE THE PROTECTOR AND PROTECT ___ FOREVER
[1. MATTER; 2. ENERGY; 3. SPACE; 4. TIME; 5. REALITY; 6. AGREEMENTS; 7. BODIES; 8. ENTITIES]

74.1 SPLIT MYSELF AND OTHERS
      INTO BINDERS FOREVER

74.2 PROGRAM MYSELF AND
      OTHERS TO BE THE BINDER
      AND BIND THE PHYSICAL
      UNIVERSE TOGETHER
      FOREVER

74.X TO {*goal*} INFINITELY IS TO BE
      THE BINDER AND ___ FOREVER
   [1. TIE THE UNIVERSE TOGETHER
INTO A COHESIVE WHOLE; 2. BIND ALL
INDIVIDUALS TOGETHER WITH THE
PHYSICAL UNIVERSE; 3. BIND ALL
INDIVIDUALS TOGETHER WITH EACH
OTHER'S INFINITE ENTITIES; 4. BIND
ALL INFINITE ENTITIES (OF ALL BEINGS)
TOGETHER; 5. BIND THE PHYSICAL
UNIVERSE TOGETHER WITH SYMBOLS;
6. BIND ALL THOUGHT TOGETHER WITH
THE PHYSICAL UNIVERSE; 7. BIND THE
PHYSICAL UNIVERSE TOGETHER WITH
THE UNIVERSE MACHINERY; 8. KEEP
THIS ALL ONE]

75.1 SPLIT MYSELF AND OTHERS
      INTO BLOCKERS FOREVER

75.2 PROGRAM MYSELF AND
      OTHERS TO BE THE BLOCKER
      AND BLOCK ALL TAMPERING
      WITH REALITY, FOREVER

75.X   TO {*goal*} INFINITELY IS TO BE
       THE BLOCKER AND ___
       FOREVER
   [1. KEEP MYSELF FROM REACHING
THE TRUE PHYSICAL UNIVERSE;
2. KEEP MY OWN EFFORTS (AS AN
INDIVIDUAL) DIRECTED AGAINST MY
OWN 'SHADOW' OF THE PHYSICAL
UNIVERSE; 3. PREVENT ANY
MANIFESTATIONS OF PSYCHOKINETICS
(telekinesis) FROM OCCURRING IN THE
TRUE PHYSICAL UNIVERSE;
4. PREVENT ANY MANIPULATION OF
REALITY BY DIRECT POSTULATE (Alpha
Thought)]

75.X   TO {*goal*} INFINITELY IS TO BE
       THE BLOCKER AND PREVENT
       MYSELF FROM REACHING THE
       ___ OF THE TRUE UNIVERSE,
       FOREVER
   [5. SPACE; 6. TIME; 7. ENERGY;
8. MATTER] {*Note: We are a few microseconds
behind the true 'Physical Universe' time.
Everything is experienced on a very slight
communication-lag. You have to reach a little
bit 'ahead' into the 'future' to contact 'Physical
Universe present-time'.*}

76.1   SPLIT MYSELF AND OTHERS

INTO CONSTRAINERS FOREVER

76.2 PROGRAM MYSELF AND
OTHERS TO BE THE
CONSTRAINER AND IMPOSE
THE LAWS OF THE PHYSICAL
UNIVERSE FOREVER

76.X TO {*goal*} INFINITELY IS TO BE
THE CONSTRAINER AND ___
FOREVER

[1. LIMIT ALL PERCEPTIONS IN
ACCORDANCE WITH PHYSICAL
UNIVERSE LAWS; 2. LIMIT ALL
MANIPULATIONS IN ACCORDANCE
WITH PHYSICAL UNIVERSE LAWS;
3. IMPOSE THE LAWS OF DISTANCE ON
ALL OPERATIONS; 4. IMPOSE THE LAWS
OF DISTORTION ON ALL OPERATIONS;
5. IMPOSE THE LAWS OF DURATION ON
ALL OPERATIONS; 6. IMPOSE THE LAWS
OF RESISTANCE ON ALL OPERATIONS;
7. IMPOSE THE LAWS OF SYMPATHY
(resonance/gravity) ON ALL OPERATIONS;
8. IMPOSE THE LAWS OF PHYSICAL
INTERACTION ON ALL OPERATIONS]

77.1 SPLIT MYSELF AND OTHERS
INTO DIFFUSERS
(DEFLECTORS) FOREVER

77.2 PROGRAM MYSELF AND
OTHERS TO BE THE

DEFLECTOR AND (?)

77.X TO {*goal*} INFINITELY IS TO BE THE DEFLECTOR AND MAKE ALL MY ___ MISS THEIR TARGETS FOREVER
   [1. BEAMS; 2. POSTULATES; (?)]

78.1 SPLIT MYSELF AND OTHERS INTO PULL-BACKS (HOLD-BACKS?) FOREVER

78.2 PROGRAM MYSELF AND OTHERS TO BE THE PULL-BACK AND (?)

78.X TO {*goal*} INFINITELY IS TO BE THE PULL-BACK AND PULL BACK ANY ___ FOREVER
   [1. ENERGY; 2. POSTULATES; 3. REACH; (?)]

79.1 SPLIT MYSELF AND OTHERS INTO VACUUMS (UNMANIFESTORS) FOREVER

79.2 PROGRAM MYSELF AND OTHERS TO BE THE VACUUM AND (?)

79.X TO {*goal*} INFINITELY IS TO BE THE VACUUM AND ___ FOREVER
   [1. MAKE THINGS UNREAL; 2. DRAIN HAVINGNESS; 3. DRAIN ENERGY;

4. CAVE THIS ALL IN ON ME; 5. PULL
EVERYTHING IN; 6. COLLAPSE
EVERYTHING; (?)]

80.1 SPLIT MYSELF AND OTHERS
INTO REFLECTORS FOREVER

80.2 PROGRAM MYSELF AND
OTHERS TO BE THE
REFLECTOR AND REFLECT
EVERYTHING BACK IN ON
MYSELF FOREVER

80.X TO {goal} INFINITELY IS TO BE
THE REFLECTOR AND REFLECT
MY ___ BACK IN ON MYSELF,
FOREVER
[1. POSTULATES; 2. ENERGY-
BEAMS; 3. BAD INTENTIONS;
4. HARMFUL-ACTS; 5. FEARS;
6. EMOTIONS; 7. CREATIONS; 8. (?)]

81.1 SPLIT MYSELF AND OTHERS
INTO GUIDES FOREVER

81.2 PROGRAM MYSELF AND
OTHERS TO BE THE GUIDE AND
LEAD MYSELF AND ALL OTHERS
DEEPER INTO THE TRAP
FOREVER

81.X TO {goal} INFINITELY IS TO BE
THE GUIDE AND ___ FOREVER
[1. LEAD MYSELF AWAY FROM TRUE

KNOWLEDGE ABOUT REALITY]

81.Y TO {goal} INFINITELY IS TO BE
THE GUIDE AND LEAD MYSELF
TOWARDS EVEN DEEPER ___
WITH THE PHYSICAL UNIVERSE,
FOREVER

[2. AFFINITY (LIKINGNESS);
3. ADMIRATION; 4. INVOLVEMENT;
5. INTEREST; 6. AGREEMENT;
7. DEPENDENCE]

81.Z TO {goal} INFINITELY IS TO BE
THE GUIDE AND LEAD ___ WITH
THE PHYSICAL UNIVERSE,
FOREVER

[8. MY INDIVIDUAL SELF TO
BECOME ONE]

82.1 SPLIT MYSELF AND OTHERS
INTO PLANNERS FOREVER

82.2 PROGRAM MYSELF AND
OTHERS TO BE THE PLANNER
AND PLAN OUT MY EXISTENCE
FOREVER

82.X TO {goal} INFINITELY IS TO BE
THE PLANNER AND ___
FOREVER

[1. KNOW THAT THE ONLY WAY OUT
IS TO GO THROUGH THE BOTTOM;
2. FIND WAYS TO KEEP MY INDIVIDUAL
SELF MOVING DOWNWARD; 3. ENJOY

DOING MYSELF IN AND SINKING DEEPER; 4. FIGURE OUT WAYS TO ENTRAP MYSELF FURTHER; 5. REFUSE TO ABANDON ANYTHING; 6. FIGURE OUT WAYS TO ENTRAP OTHERS; 7. FIGHT BACK AGAINST ANYONE WHO TRIES TO GET ME OUT; 8. LEAD MYSELF DOWN THE DECLINING SPIRAL]

83.1 SPLIT MYSELF AND OTHERS INTO GAME-MAKERS FOREVER

83.2 PROGRAM MYSELF AND OTHERS TO BE THE GAME-MAKER AND (?)

83.X TO {*goal*} INFINITELY IS TO BE THE GAME-MAKER AND (?)

84.1 SPLIT MYSELF AND OTHERS INTO GOAL-MAKERS FOREVER

84.2 PROGRAM MYSELF AND OTHERS TO BE THE GOAL-MAKER AND (?)

84.X TO {*goal*} INFINITELY IS TO BE THE GOAL-MAKER AND (?)

85.1 SPLIT MYSELF AND OTHERS INTO FUTURIZERS FOREVER

85.2 PROGRAM MYSELF AND OTHERS TO BE THE FUTURIZER AND PROJECT (CREATE) A

FUTURE FOR MYSELF (AND
OTHERS?) FOREVER

85.X TO {goal} INFINITELY IS TO BE
THE FUTURIZER AND PROJECT
___ FOR MYSELF INTO THE
PHYSICAL UNIVERSE FUTURE,
FOREVER

[1. GAMES; 2. IDENTITIES; 3.
ACTIVITIES; 4. HAVINGNESS; 5. GOALS;
6. EXPECTATIONS; 7. CONSEQUENCES;
8. MY OWN PERPETUAL EXISTENCE]

86.1 SPLIT MYSELF AND OTHERS
INTO ENCOURAGERS FOREVER

86.2 PROGRAM MYSELF AND
OTHERS TO BE THE
ENCOURAGER AND
ENCOURAGE MYSELF TO
ACHIEVE THINGS IN THE
PHYSICAL UNIVERSE FOREVER

86.X TO {goal} INFINITELY IS TO BE
THE ENCOURAGER AND
ENCOURAGE MYSELF TO
STRIVE ___ IN THE PHYSICAL
UNIVERSE FOREVER

[1. FOR ETHICS; 2. FOR
AESTHETICS; 3. TO BUILD THINGS;
4. FOR LOGIC AND REASON; 5. FOR
CHANCE; 6. FOR GAMES; 7. FOR
KNOWLEDGE; 8. TO CREATE THINGS]

87.1 SPLIT MYSELF AND OTHERS
INTO COACHES FOREVER

87.2 PROGRAM MYSELF AND
OTHERS TO BE THE COACH & ?

87.X TO {*goal*} INFINITELY IS TO BE
THE COACH AND (?)

{false data is to 'keep myself from winning
or losing' to 'make games go on forever'}

88.1 SPLIT MYSELF AND OTHERS
INTO ALIGNERS
(COORDINATORS) FOREVER

88.2 PROGRAM MYSELF AND
OTHERS TO BE THE ALIGNER
AND (?)

88.X TO {*goal*} INFINITELY IS TO BE
THE ALIGNER AND (?)

89.1 SPLIT MYSELF AND OTHERS
INTO WATCHERS (MONITORS)
FOREVER

89.2 PROGRAM MYSELF AND
OTHERS TO BE THE WATCHER
AND MONITOR (WATCH) ALL OF
THIS FOREVER

89.X TO {*goal*} INFINITELY IS TO BE
THE WATCHER AND ___
FOREVER

[1. WATCH ALL THE OTHERS TO
ENSURE THAT THEY ARE OBEYING

249

ORDERS; 2. OBSERVE MYSELF AS AN INDIVIDUAL TO ENSURE THAT I REMAIN ENTRAPPED BY THIS; 3. OBSERVE PHYSICAL REALITY TO ENSURE THAT IT REMAINS INVIOLATE; 4. WATCH THE MECHANICS BEHIND REALITY TO ENSURE THAT THEY CONTINUE TO WORK]

89.Y TO {goal} INFINITELY IS TO BE THE WATCHER AND REPORT ANY ___ TO THE OTHER ENTITIES (OVERSOULS?) FOREVER

[5. VIOLATIONS OF THESE ORDERS; 6. ATTEMPTS TO UNMANIFEST (UNCREATE) THIS; 7. VIOLATIONS OF REALITY; 8. FAILURES OF THESE MECHANISMS]

90.1 SPLIT MYSELF AND OTHERS INTO EQUALIZERS FOREVER

90.2 PROGRAM MYSELF AND OTHERS TO BE THE EQUALIZER AND (?)

90.X TO {goal} INFINITELY IS TO BE THE EQUALIZER AND (?)

91.1 SPLIT MYSELF AND OTHERS INTO OPPOSERS FOREVER

91.2 PROGRAM MYSELF AND

OTHERS TO BE THE OPPOSER
AND (?)

91.X TO {goal} INFINITELY IS TO BE
THE OPPOSER AND (?)

92.1 SPLIT MYSELF AND OTHERS
INTO DECEIVERS FOREVER

92.2 PROGRAM MYSELF AND
OTHERS TO BE THE DECEIVER
AND DECEIVE MYSELF
FOREVER

92.X TO {goal} INFINITELY IS TO BE
THE DECEIVER AND DECEIVE
MYSELF AS TO THE ___
FOREVER

[1. NATURE OF REALITY; 2. NATURE
OF OTHER BEINGS; 3. NATURE OF
LIFEFORMS; 4. ANATOMY OF THE
PHYSICAL UNIVERSE; 5. ORIGINS OF
THE PHYSICAL UNIVERSE; 6. ORIGINS
OF MYSELF; 7. (?); 8. ORDERS
CONCERNING FOREVER]

93.1 SPLIT MYSELF AND OTHERS
INTO INVERTERS FOREVER

93.2 PROGRAM MYSELF AND
OTHERS TO BE THE INVERTER
AND (?)

93.X TO {goal} INFINITELY IS TO BE
THE INVERTER AND (?)

94.1 SPLIT MYSELF AND OTHERS
      INTO DISPERSERS FOREVER
94.2 PROGRAM MYSELF AND
      OTHERS TO BE THE DISPERSER
      AND DISPERSE ANY ENERGY
      THAT I PUT OUT, FOREVER
94.X TO {*goal*} INFINITELY IS TO BE
      THE DISPERSER AND DISPERSE
      ___, FOREVER
   [1. ENERGY-BEAMS; 2. POSTULATES;
3. INTENTIONS; 4. ATTENTION; 5.
CONCENTRATION; 6. ANCHOR-POINTS;
7. VIEWPOINTS; 8. PROGRAMMING]
{item-8 may be 'vibrations'?}

95.1 SPLIT MYSELF AND OTHERS
      INTO FATES (ARRANGERS)
      FOREVER
95.2 PROGRAM MYSELF AND
      OTHERS TO BE THE ARRANGER
      AND ARRANGE FATES FOR
      MYSELF, FOREVER
95.X TO {*goal*} INFINITELY IS TO BE
      THE ARRANGER AND ARRANGE
      ___ FOR MYSELF, FOREVER
   [1. EVENTS; 2. (?);
3. CIRCUMSTANCES; (?)]

96.1 SPLIT MYSELF AND OTHERS
      INTO TRICKSTERS FOREVER

252

96.2 PROGRAM MYSELF AND OTHERS TO BE THE TRICKSTER AND TRICK MYSELF FOREVER

96.X TO {goal} INFINITELY IS TO BE THE TRICKSTER AND (GO AROUND AND) FOOL MYSELF AS TO ___, FOREVER

[1. WHO IS REALLY DOING THINGS; 2. WHEN THINGS REALLY HAPPENED; 3. WHAT IS REALLY GOING ON; 4. THE ACTUAL PURPOSE BEHIND THINGS; 5. THE ACTUAL ORIGINS OF THINGS; 6. HOW THINGS REALLY WORK; 7. THE ACTUAL STRUCTURE OF THINGS; 8. WHO I REALLY AM]

97.1 SPLIT MYSELF AND OTHERS INTO 'PARTS OF GOD' (CREATORS) FOREVER

97.2 PROGRAM MYSELF AND OTHERS TO BE THE CREATOR AND CREATE THIS FOREVER

97.X TO {goal} INFINITELY IS TO BE THE CREATOR AND CREATE ___ FOREVER

[1. MYSELF AS AN INDIVIDUAL; 2. BODIES; 3. OTHER INDIVIDUALS; 4. SOCIETIES; 5. LIFEFORMS; 6. THE PHYSICAL UNIVERSE; 7. ENTITIES; 8. UNIVERSAL MIND]

{'Universal Mind' also registers as separate
item? Experimental data given below.}

97B. TO {*goal*} INFINITELY IS TO BE
THE UNIVERSAL MIND AND ___
THE PHYSICAL UNIVERSE
FOREVER
[1. BE THE THOUGHT OF; 2. THINK
ON BEHALF OF; 3. ARRANGE FOR THE
SURVIVAL OF; 4. THINK ABOUT]

97C. TO {*goal*} INFINITELY IS TO BE
THE UNIVERSAL MIND AND ___
ALL THESE OTHERS, FOREVER
[1. BE; 2. HIDE THE THOUGHTS OF;
3. HOLD TOGETHER THE THOUGHTS
OF; 4. FORGET THE THOUGHTS OF;
5. PROTECT THE THOUGHTS OF]

98.1 SPLIT MYSELF AND OTHERS
INTO ANGELS FOREVER

98.2 PROGRAM MYSELF AND
OTHERS TO BE THE ANGEL AND
HELP 'GOD' FOREVER

{Note that here, 'god' is a construct that
acts as a 'mind' for the Universe; you
give a piece of yourself to its service.}

98.X TO {*goal*} INFINITELY IS TO BE
THE ANGEL AND ___ FOREVER
[1. SERVE GOD; 2. CARRY OUT THE
ORDERS OF GOD; 3. OBEY THE WISHES

OF GOD; 4. MAINTAIN THE LAWS OF GOD; 5. ENACT THE PLANS OF GOD; 6. AGREE WITH THE MANIFESTATIONS (CREATIONS/MOCK-UPS) OF GOD; 7. SEE TO THE NEEDS OF GOD; 8. GRANT POWER (over your individual self) UNTO GOD]

99.1 SPLIT MYSELF AND OTHERS INTO ATTRACTORS FOREVER

99.2 PROGRAM MYSELF AND OTHERS TO BE THE ATTRACTOR AND COMPEL MYSELF TO NEED THE PHYSICAL UNIVERSE FOREVER

99.X TO {*goal*} INFINITELY IS TO BE THE ATTRACTOR AND COMPEL MYSELF TO ___ FOREVER

[1. HAVE AFFINITY (LIKINGNESS) FOR THE PHYSICAL UNIVERSE; 2. BE IN AGREEMENT WITH THE PHYSICAL UNIVERSE; 3. BE IN COMMUNICATION WITH THE PHYSICAL UNIVERSE; 4. HAVE ADMIRATION FOR THE PHYSICAL UNIVERSE; 5. DEPEND ON THE PHYSICAL UNIVERSE FOR AFFINITY (LIKINGNESS); 6. DEPEND ON THE PHYSICAL UNIVERSE FOR REALITY; 7. DEPEND ON THE PHYSICAL UNIVERSE FOR COMMUNICATION;

8. DEPEND ON THE PHYSICAL
UNIVERSE FOR ADMIRATION]

100.1 SPLIT MYSELF AND OTHERS
INTO ACCUSERS FOREVER

100.2 PROGRAM MYSELF AND
OTHERS TO BE THE ACCUSER
AND (?)

100.X TO {goal} INFINITELY IS TO BE
THE ACCUSER AND (?)

101.1 SPLIT MYSELF AND OTHERS
INTO JUDGES FOREVER

101.2 PROGRAM MYSELF AND
OTHERS TO BE THE JUDGE AND
JUDGE MYSELF, FOREVER

101.X TO {goal} INFINITELY IS TO BE
THE JUDGE AND CONDEMN
(BLAME) MYSELF FOR ___
FOREVER

[1. ALL MY FAILINGS; 2. ALL THE
HARM I HAVE DONE; 3. ALL THE WRONG
THOUGHTS THAT I HAVE HAD; 4. ALL MY
WEAKNESSES]

101.Y TO {goal} INFINITELY IS TO BE
THE JUDGE AND ARRANGE ___
FOREVER

[5. PUNISHMENTS FOR MY
MISDEEDS; 6. FOR MY DEEDS TO COME
BACK ON ME; 7. LESSONS FOR MYSELF

TO TEACH ME TO BE GOOD; 8. FATES
FOR MYSELF TO PUNISH MY CRIMES]

102.1 SPLIT MYSELF AND OTHERS
INTO PUNISHERS FOREVER

102.2 PROGRAM MYSELF AND
OTHERS TO BE THE PUNISHER
AND (?)

102.X TO {*goal*} INFINITELY IS TO BE
THE PUNISHER AND (?)

103.1 SPLIT MYSELF AND OTHERS
INTO EXECUTIONERS FOREVER

103.2 PROGRAM MYSELF AND
OTHERS TO BE THE
EXECUTIONER AND (?)

103.X TO {*goal*} INFINITELY IS TO BE
THE EXECUTIONER AND (?)

104.1 SPLIT MYSELF AND OTHERS
INTO RECYCLERS FOREVER

104.2 PROGRAM MYSELF AND
OTHERS TO BE THE RECYCLER
AND REFORMAT MYSELF
BETWEEN LIVES FOREVER

104.X TO {*goal*} INFINITELY IS TO BE
THE RECYCLER AND
RESTRUCTURE MY ___
BETWEEN LIVES FOREVER
[1. PERSONALITY; 2. MEMORIES;

3. ABILITIES; 4. BEINGNESS (IDENTITY)]

104.Y TO {goal} INFINITELY IS TO BE
THE RECYCLER AND
FORMULATE FOR MYSELF ___
BETWEEN LIVES FOREVER
[5. NEW GOALS; 6. NEW LESSONS;
7. NEW CHALLENGES; 8. NEW
ABERRATIONS]

105.1 SPLIT MYSELF AND OTHERS
INTO INTERIORIZERS FOREVER

105.2 PROGRAM MYSELF AND
OTHERS TO BE THE
INTERIORIZER AND (?)

105.X TO {goal} INFINITELY IS TO BE
THE INTERIORIZER AND (?)

106.1 SPLIT MYSELF AND OTHERS
INTO DISCOURAGERS FOREVER

106.2 PROGRAM MYSELF AND
OTHERS TO BE THE
DISCOURAGER AND CONVINCE
MYSELF AND OTHERS THAT
NOTHING CAN BE DONE ABOUT
THIS FOREVER

106.X TO {goal} INFINITELY IS TO BE
THE DISCOURAGER AND
DISCOURAGE MYSELF AND
OTHERS FROM EVER DOING
ANYTHING ABOUT ___ FOREVER

[1. THIS IMPLANT; 2. ENTITIES;
3. THE PHYSICAL UNIVERSE; 4. THE
SPLITTER MECHANISMS]

106.Y TO {*goal*} INFINITELY IS TO BE
        THE DISCOURAGER AND
        CONVINCE MYSELF AND
        OTHERS THAT ___ FOREVER
    [5. THIS IS TOO SOLID TO BE TAKEN
APART; 6. EVEN IF THIS COULD BE
TAKEN APART (ERASED) IT WOULD NOT
MAKE ANY DIFFERENCE ANYWAY;
7. EVEN IF YOU COULD TAKE THIS ALL
APART, YOU WOULDN'T WANT TO;
8. EVEN IF YOU DID TAKE THIS ALL
APART, YOU WOULD SUFFER A LOSS
AND BE SORRY THAT YOU HAD DONE
IT] {'Discourager' may be the same as item-
    27 'Depressor'?}

107.1 SPLIT MYSELF AND OTHERS
        INTO CONFUSION-ENTITIES
        FOREVER
107.2 PROGRAM MYSELF AND
        OTHERS TO BE THE
        CONFUSION ENTITY AND KEEP
        MYSELF CONFUSED FOREVER
107.X TO {*goal*} INFINITELY IS TO BE
        THE CONFUSION ENTITY AND
        CONFUSE ___ (SO THAT THEY

259

CAN NEVER BE SORTED OUT)
FOREVER

[1. TRUTH WITH FALSEHOOD; 2.
REALITY WITH UNREALITY; 3. MYSELF
WITH OTHERS; 4. PAST WITH PRESENT;
5. TIME WITH SPACE; 6. MATTER WITH
ENERGY; 7. IDENTITY WITH LOCATION;
8. IMPACT WITH ENLIGHTENMENT]

108.1 SPLIT MYSELF AND OTHERS
       INTO TERROR (FEAR) ENTITIES
       FOREVER

108.2 PROGRAM MYSELF AND
       OTHERS TO BE THE TERROR
       ENTITY AND TERRIFY MYSELF
       FOREVER

108.X TO {goal} INFINITELY IS TO BE
       THE TERROR ENTITY AND ___
       FOREVER

[1. MANIFEST (MOCK-UP)
MONSTERS AND DEMONS;
2. TERRORIZE MYSELF]

108.Y TO {goal} INFINITELY IS TO BE
       THE TERROR ENTITY AND MAKE
       MYSELF AFRAID TO ___
       FOREVER

[3. FIND OUT THE TRUTH; 4. SEE
ENTITIES; 5. SEE ANY DISCREPANCY IN
REALITY; 6. SEE ANY VIOLATION OF
REALITY; 7. REMEMBER ANYTHING

BEFORE THIS UNIVERSE; 8. DISCOVER
ANY PART OF THESE MECHANISMS]

109.1 SPLIT MYSELF AND OTHERS
       INTO DELUSION-ENTITIES
       FOREVER

109.2 PROGRAM MYSELF AND
       OTHERS TO BE THE DELUSION
       ENTITY AND CREATE
       DELUSIONS FOR MYSELF
       FOREVER

109.X TO {*goal*} INFINITELY IS TO BE
       THE DELUSION ENTITY AND ___
       FOREVER

    [1. DELUDE MYSELF AS TO THE
TRUE NATURE OF REALITY; 2. CREATE
FALSE REALITIES FOR MYSELF; 3. DUB-
IN FALSE PERCEPTIONS; 4. DUB-IN
MISCONCEPTIONS ABOUT REALITY;
5. DUB-IN INCORRECT CONCLUSIONS;
6. DUB-IN WRONG REASONS WHY;
7. CONVINCE MYSELF THAT ENTITIES
ARE DELUSIONS; 8. CONVINCE MYSELF
THAT PERCEPTIONS OF THE REAL
NATURE OF REALITY ARE DELUSIONS]

110.1 SPLIT MYSELF AND OTHERS
       INTO DEGRADERS FOREVER

110.2 PROGRAM MYSELF AND
       OTHERS TO BE THE DEGRADER

AND DEGRADE MYSELF
FOREVER

110.x   TO {goal} INFINITELY IS TO BE
THE DEGRADER AND INSPIRE
MYSELF TO BE ___ FOREVER
[1. GREEDY; 2. LUSTFUL; 3. CRUEL;
4. DISHONEST; 5. LAZY; 6. VISCOUS
(NASTY); 7. SELFISH; 8. VENGEFUL]

111.1   SPLIT MYSELF AND OTHERS
INTO TEMPTERS FOREVER

111.2   PROGRAM MYSELF AND
OTHERS TO BE THE TEMPTER
AND (?)

111.x   TO {goal} INFINITELY IS TO BE
THE TEMPTER AND (?)

112.1   SPLIT MYSELF AND OTHERS
INTO DEMONS (DEVILS)
FOREVER

112.2   PROGRAM MYSELF AND
OTHERS TO BE THE DEMON
AND MAKE TROUBLE FOR
MYSELF FOREVER
{'entrap myself forever'?}

112.x   TO {goal} INFINITELY IS TO BE
THE DEMON AND CREATE ___
FOR MYSELF, FOREVER
[1. PROBLEMS; 2. DIFFICULTIES;
3. UPSETS; 4. LOSSES; 5. GUILT;

6. PENALTIES; 7. TRAPS; 8. DECLINING SPIRALS]

{'Devil' also registers as separate item? Experimental data given below.}

112A. TO {*goal*} INFINITELY IS TO BE THE DEVIL AND INSPIRE MYSELF TOWARDS EVIL WITHIN THE PHYSICAL UNIVERSE, FOREVER

112B. TO {*goal*} INFINITELY IS TO BE THE DEVIL AND MAKE TROUBLE BETWEEN MYSELF AND ___, FOREVER

[1. OTHERS; 2. SOCIETY; 3. GOD; 4. THE PHYSICAL UNIVERSE]

113.1 SPLIT MYSELF AND OTHERS INTO INNER-GUARDS FOREVER

113.2 PROGRAM MYSELF AND OTHERS TO BE THE INNER-GUARD AND STOP MYSELF FROM KNOWING ABOUT MYSELF, FOREVER

113.X TO {*goal*} INFINITELY IS TO BE THE INNER-GUARD AND MAKE MYSELF AFRAID TO ___, FOREVER

[1. SEE MYSELF; 2. FIND OUT WHERE I REALLY AM; 3. FIND OUT WHO

I REALLY AM; 4. FIND OUT WHAT I
REALLY AM; 5. FIND OUT WHEN I
REALLY AM; 6. FIND OUT MY TRUE
NATURE; 7. FIND OUT MY TRUE
ORIGINS; 8. LOOK INWARD]

114.1   SPLIT MYSELF AND OTHERS
        INTO DRAMATIZERS FOREVER
114.2   PROGRAM MYSELF AND
        OTHERS TO BE THE
        DRAMATIZER AND (?)
114.X   TO {*goal*} INFINITELY IS TO BE
        THE DRAMATIZER AND (?)

115.1   SPLIT MYSELF AND OTHERS
        INTO PERPETUATORS FOREVER
115.2   PROGRAM MYSELF AND
        OTHERS TO BE THE
        PERPETUATOR AND (?)
115.X   TO {*goal*} INFINITELY IS TO BE
        THE PERPETUATOR AND (?)

116.1   SPLIT MYSELF AND OTHERS
        INTO CORRECTIVE-MACHINERY
        FOREVER
116.2   PROGRAM MYSELF AND
        OTHERS TO BE THE
        CORRECTIVE MACHINE-ENTITY
        AND KEEP THIS ALL WORKING
        FOREVER

116.X TO {*goal*} INFINITELY IS TO BE
        THE CORRECTIVE-ENTITY AND
        ___, FOREVER
    [1. REMEDY ANY DISCREPANCIES
IN REALITY; 2. ALTER PERCEPTIONS TO
KEEP REALITY CONSISTENT AND HIDE
ANY DISCREPANCIES; 3. ALTER
MEMORY TO KEEP REALITY
CONSISTENT AND HIDE ANY
DISCREPANCIES; 4. MAKE MYSELF AND
OTHERS SPLIT TO REPLACE ANY
ENTITIES THAT ARE RELEASED
{registers, but may be part of item-117};
5. USE THE RESOURCES OF ALL THESE
OTHERS TO REPROGRAM ANY PART OF
THIS IMPLANT THAT FAILS;
6. CONVINCE MYSELF AND OTHERS TO
OBEY THIS IMPLANT; 7. USE THE
RESOURCES OF ALL THESE OTHERS
TO KEEP THIS CONTINUOUSLY
CREATED; 8. REPORT ALL
INFRACTIONS TO THE OVERSOULS]

117.1 SPLIT MYSELF AND OTHERS
        INTO SPLITTERS FOREVER
117.2 PROGRAM MYSELF AND
        OTHERS TO BE THE SPLITTER
        AND (?)
117.X TO {*goal*} INFINITELY IS TO BE

THE SPLITTER AND (?)

118.1 SPLIT MYSELF AND OTHERS INTO IMPLANTERS FOREVER

118.2 PROGRAM MYSELF AND OTHERS TO BE THE IMPLANTER AND IMPLANT MYSELF WITH ORDERS AS AN INDIVIDUAL, FOREVER

{wording may be '..myself as an individual, with orders,..'}

118.X TO {goal} INFINITELY IS TO BE THE IMPLANTER AND IMPLANT MYSELF (WITH ORDERS) TO ___ FOREVER

[1. BELIEVE IN REALITY; 2. AGREE WITH REALITY; 3. BE THE EFFECT OF (or 'affected by') REALITY; 4. BE LOCATED WITHIN REALITY (or 'the Physical Universe'); 5. BELIEVE THAT THE PHYSICAL UNIVERSE IS LARGER ('greater') THAN I AM; 6. BELIEVE THAT THE PHYSICAL UNIVERSE IS MORE IMPORTANT THAN I AM; 7. BELIEVE THAT THE PHYSICAL UNIVERSE IS MORE POWERFUL THAN I AM; 8. BELIEVE THAT THE PHYSICAL UNIVERSE IS MORE ENDURING THAN I AM]

119.1 SPLIT MYSELF AND OTHERS INTO KEEPERS FOREVER

119.2 PROGRAM MYSELF AND OTHERS TO BE THE KEEPER AND (?)

119.X TO {*goal*} INFINITELY IS TO BE THE KEEPER AND (?)

120.1 SPLIT MYSELF AND OTHERS INTO UNIFIERS (JOINERS) FOREVER

120.2 PROGRAM MYSELF AND OTHERS TO BE THE UNIFIER AND MAKE EVERYTHING ONE FOREVER

120.X TO {*goal*} INFINITELY IS TO BE THE UNIFIER AND BE ONE WITH ___, FOREVER
[1. INFINITY; 2. ALL THESE ENTITIES; 3. THE PHYSICAL UNIVERSE; 4. ALL LIFEFORMS; 5. ALL SOCIETIES; 6. ALL OTHER INDIVIDUALS; 7. BODIES; 8. THE ITEMS OF THIS IMPLANT]

121.1 SPLIT MYSELF AND OTHERS INTO RESTIMULATORS FOREVER

121.2 PROGRAM MYSELF AND OTHERS TO BE THE RESTIMULATOR AND KEEP THIS

IN RESTIMULATION FOREVER

121.X TO {goal} INFINITELY IS TO BE THE RESTIMULATOR AND ___, FOREVER

[1. CREATE THIS IMPLANT CONTINUOUSLY; 2. FORCE MYSELF AND OTHERS TO CROSS-COPY INFINITELY; 3. FORCE MYSELF AND OTHERS TO DIVIDE INFINITELY; 4. FORCE MYSELF AND OTHERS TO DRAMATIZE THIS; 5. REPEAT THE ITEMS OF THIS IMPLANT; 6. FORCE MYSELF AND OTHERS TO REMAIN THE EFFECT OF THIS; 7. KEEP THIS IMPLANT SOLID; 8. RE-CREATE THE IMPACT OF THIS INCIDENT]

122.1 SPLIT MYSELF AND OTHERS INTO INVALIDATORS FOREVER

122.2 PROGRAM MYSELF AND OTHERS TO BE THE INVALIDATOR AND INVALIDATE ANY AWARENESS OF THIS IMPLANT, FOREVER

122.X TO {goal} INFINITELY IS TO BE THE INVALIDATOR AND INVALIDATE ANY ___ OF THIS IMPLANT, FOREVER

[1. AWARENESS; 2. KNOWLEDGE; 3. REMEMBRANCE; 4. UNDERSTANDING;

5. ERASURE OF; 6. FREEDOM FROM; 7. COMMAND OVER; 8. MASTERY OF]

123.1 SPLIT MYSELF AND OTHERS INTO MISDIRECTORS FOREVER

123.2 PROGRAM MYSELF AND OTHERS TO BE THE MISDIRECTOR AND MISLEAD ANYONE WHO ATTEMPTS TO DISCOVER THIS, FOREVER

123.X TO {*goal*} INFINITELY IS TO BE THE MISDIRECTOR AND ___, FOREVER

[1. SUBSTITUTE WRONG DATES CONCERNING THE BACKTRACK; 2. MAKE MYSELF AND OTHERS CONFUSE THE CORRECT SEQUENCE OF EVENTS; 3. MANUFACTURE FALSE-DATA; 4. MAKE MYSELF AND OTHERS MIX UP LOCATIONS; 5. MAKE MYSELF AND OTHERS DUB-IN IMAGINARY INCIDENTS; 6. MISLEAD MYSELF AND OTHERS; 7. DIRECT ATTENTION AWAY FROM THIS INCIDENT; 8. PREVENT THE TRUTH FROM BEING DISCOVERED]

124.1 SPLIT MYSELF AND OTHERS INTO DENIERS FOREVER

124.2 PROGRAM MYSELF AND OTHERS TO BE THE DENIER

AND DENY THE EXISTENCE OF
THIS FOREVER

124.X TO {goal} INFINITELY IS TO BE
THE DENIER AND ___ FOREVER

[1. INSIST THAT ENTITIES DO NOT
EXIST; 2. INSIST THAT INFINITY DOES
NOT EXIST; 3. DENY THAT ANY OF THIS
IS REAL; 4. DENY THAT THIS EVER
HAPPENED; 5. INVALIDATE THE
REALITY OF ANY NON-PHYSICAL
UNIVERSE MANIFESTATION ('creation' or
'mock-up'); 6. INSIST THAT THE
PHYSICAL UNIVERSE IS THE ONLY
REALITY; 7. COMPEL MYSELF AND
OTHERS TO DISBELIEVE IN THE
EXISTENCE OF THIS IMPLANT;
8. COMPEL MYSELF AND OTHERS TO
DISBELIEVE IN THE EXISTENCE OF THE
INFINITE {terminal}]

125.1 SPLIT MYSELF AND OTHERS
INTO SUPPRESSORS FOREVER

125.2 PROGRAM MYSELF AND
OTHERS TO BE THE
SUPPRESSOR AND KEEP THIS
HIDDEN FOREVER

125.X TO {goal} INFINITELY IS TO BE
THE SUPPRESSOR AND KEEP
MYSELF FROM ___ THIS
FOREVER

[1. SPOTTING; 2. KNOWING ABOUT; 3. PERCEIVING; 4. COMMUNICATING ABOUT; 5. THINKING ABOUT]

125.Y TO {goal} INFINITELY IS TO BE THE SUPPRESSOR AND ___ FOREVER

[6. KEEP THIS FROM REGISTERING ON ANY DETECTION-DEVICES; 7. STOP THIS FROM BEING DISCOVERED; 8. USE THE RESOURCES OF ALL THESE OTHER ENTITIES TO BLOCK ALL KNOWLEDGE OF THIS]

126.1 SPLIT MYSELF AND OTHERS INTO HOLDERS FOREVER

126.2 PROGRAM MYSELF AND OTHERS TO BE THE HOLDER AND HOLD EVERYONE TOGETHER FOREVER

126.X TO {goal} INFINITELY IS TO BE THE HOLDER AND ___, FOREVER

[1. MAKE EVERYONE ALL ONE; 2. JOIN EVERYONE TOGETHER; 3. HOLD EVERYONE IN A SINGLE REALITY; 4. COMBINE EVERYONE INTO A SINGLE BEING; 5. MAKE EVERYONE HOLD ON TO EACH OTHER; 6. HOLD MYSELF AND OTHERS IN AGREEMENT TOGETHER; 7. HOLD ON TO ALL THESE

BEINGS; 8. KEEP ANYONE FROM LEAVING]

127.1 SPLIT MYSELF AND OTHERS INTO GUARDIANS FOREVER

127.2 PROGRAM MYSELF AND OTHERS TO BE THE GUARDIAN AND PROTECT THIS IMPLANT (FROM BEING VIEWED), FOREVER

127.X TO {goal} INFINITELY IS TO BE THE GUARDIAN AND PREVENT MYSELF AND OTHERS FROM ___ FOREVER

[1. VIOLATING THE RULES OF THE PHYSICAL UNIVERSE; 2. MOVING OUT OF THE PHYSICAL UNIVERSE; 3. MODIFYING REALITY; 4. FINDING OUT THE TRUTH ABOUT REALITY; 5. CHANGING THE NATURE OF REALITY; 6. DISAGREEING WITH REALITY; 7. KNOWING THAT I AM DOING THESE THINGS; 8. REMEMBERING THIS IMPLANT]

128.1 SPLIT MYSELF AND OTHERS INTO OVERSOULS FOREVER

128.2 PROGRAM MYSELF AND OTHERS TO BE THE OVERSOUL AND ORGANIZE ALL THESE

OTHERS FOREVER

128.X TO {*goal*} INFINITELY IS TO BE
       THE OVERSOUL AND ___
       FOREVER
   [1. MANAGE THIS; 2. SEE THAT THIS
IS REPAIRED; 3. COORDINATE ALL
THESE OTHERS; 4. ORGANIZE MYSELF
AND ALL THESE OTHERS; 5. CONTROL
MYSELF AND ALL THESE OTHERS;
6. KEEP MYSELF AND ALL THESE
OTHERS DIVIDED; 7. LIE ABOUT THIS
TO MYSELF AND ALL THESE OTHERS;
8. KEEP MYSELF AND ALL THESE
OTHERS ENTRAPPED]

ADDITIONAL RESEARCH NOTES:

Other entity type-labels may include a *Problem-Maker*; and also a *Balancer, Equalizer,* or *Tabulator (for karma)*. Or these may be alternate labels for existing types on the list that require more research.

There is some *Meter-data* for a *Convincer*, to "convince myself that I need this" or "make myself dependent on this," *&tc*. The label *"Misleader"* also registers; but may be similar to (or the same as) the

"*Guide*" —that "guides my individual self deeper into the Physical Universe, forever," and "keep myself more in agreement," "keep myself more confused," "more solid," *&tc*. More research is needed to be certain.

There are also additional "*Higher-Self*" *items* that apply to the ending sequence of the *Implant*. These have already been well researched; however, their precise wording and sequencing is still in question.

1. MAKE THIS ALL HAPPEN (FOREVER); 2. REMAIN IN AGREEMENT WITH THIS IMPLANT (FOREVER); 3. KEEP THIS ALL WORKING (FOREVER); 4. KEEP THIS ALL IN MOTION (FOREVER); 5. NEVER LET MY LOWER SELF KNOW WHAT I AM DOING (FOREVER); 6. RULE OVER ALL THESE OTHER (ENTITIES) (FOREVER); 5. ENJOY DOING THIS (FOREVER); 7. ENJOY BEING HERE (FOREVER); 8. NEVER THINK ABOUT BEING HERE (FOREVER).

SECTION 5. FINAL ITEMS

TO {goal} INFINITELY IS TO BE ALL THESE THINGS AND ___, FOREVER

1. BLOCK ALL AWARENESS OF THESE ORDERS
2. BLOCK ALL KNOWLEDGE OF INFINITY
3. BLOCK ALL REMEMBRANCE OF THIS
4. BLOCK ALL KNOWLEDGE OF THESE ENTITIES
5. KEEP MYSELF AND OTHERS UNKNOWING
6. KEEP MYSELF AND OTHERS ASLEEP
7. KEEP MYSELF AND OTHERS UNCONSCIOUS
8. KEEP MYSELF AND OTHERS DEAD

SECTION 6. FINAL PROCESSING STEPS

Use these methods for "group-processing" any entities remaining after completing the Splitter-Platform (incident-sequence) given in previous sections. Apply as many techniques as is necessary to resolve the case.

A. *Imagine* "doing" and "not doing" (alternately) these things repeatedly to an *end-point*.

B. *Spot* "being programmed into being" these things. *Spot* the first time. *Spot* programming others. *Spot* others programming others.

C. *Spot* "being made to split." *Spot* first time; to others; others to others.

D. *Spot* "being implanted with false-data." *Spot* first time; to others; others to others.

E. *Spot* "being made to divide out to infinity." *Spot* first time; to others; others to others.

F. *Spot* "being made into the infinite {*terminal*}." *Spot* first time; to others; others to others.

G. *Decide* "to be" and "not be" the *infinite-terminal* (alternately) repeatedly to an *end-point*.

H. *Imagine* "creating" and "un-creating" the *infinite-terminal* (alternately) until you are at *Cause* over it.

I. *Spot* "the first item of the *Splitter-Platform*" (*To {goal} Infinitely Is To Perceive Ultimate Truth*); *Spot* it as *false-data*.

J. *Spot* the "*Native State*" *item* for the IPU-*Goal*. *Spot* being pushed into it; pushing others into it; others pushing others into it.

K. Ask the entity: "*Can You Create?*" It will *register* as "*yes*" on the *GSR-Meter*. If not: have the *entity* practice *imagining/creating* and "*throwing away*" a few objects; then ask again.

L. Ask the entity: "*Are You Free Of This?*" If it does not *register*: *list* to find out why (what *item* is not fully *discharged*).

M. *Identification Tech.* (*Who Are You?*)

N. *Locational Tech.* (*Point To..*)

Then check if anything remains to be handled—if any *entities* didn't *release*, &tc. Other *entities*, from other *Goals*, may try to "copy" and "replace" what was just handled. So, check for that; and if it is the case, simply indicate it to yourself (it *disperses-on-realization*).

Then *process-out* the IPU-*Platform* (*AT#4*) to *total defragmentation* on that *Goal*. Since you've handled the *Splitter-Incident*, the *defragmentation* may occur relatively quickly after a small number of *items*.

Only after this point should you handle the *negative-Goals*. When you do: start by *spotting* the "*Native State*" *item* of the *basic (positive)* IPU-*Goal*. Then, reaffirm (to yourself) the *total defragmentation* of the *basic-Goal* by *spotting* the point (in time) when you *totally defragmented* it with the *Platform*. Do this any time you feel that "*charge*" may be accumulating on the *basic* while handling the *negative*.

OPENING GATES TO THE KINGDOM
(*The Beginning In The Ending*)

A *Wizard* is one who is not only a *Master* of their own *Universe*, but who has the ability and certainty to knowingly affect and change the *Universe* around them; for themselves, and for others. We are not speaking of stage acts and parlor tricks; we mean actually *helping one another* and *making this world a better place* to conduct our *Ascension* work.

For the first time in known history (including the *Backtrack*), there is a true launch point toward *Ascension* available to humanity—and *it is our Systemology*. As should be self-evident after *33* progressive *lesson-booklets* and *manuals*: all of this could have only been uncovered with a *Self-Honest systematic approach*.

The basic *spiritual cartography* is complete

—and the *Way Out* has been cleared. Are there still some rough patches that require additional development? Sure. But, that is where you come in—investing yourself in the final *research-actions* necessary for your own *Ascension*; and perhaps assisting your fellow *Seekers* by contributing to the ongoing *Infinity Grade* that is intended to follow hereafter and preserve the legacy of the *Systemology Society* and the perfection of its knowledge.

This presentation of the final *Keys to the Kingdom* volume—and the completion of an entire library synthesizing the *systematic truth* of *spiritual life* and *all existence*—marks the end of a personal *29-year quest*. Bearing the weight of carrying *Excalibur* —the *Sword of Truth* or *Sword of Shannara* —to *dispel all illusion*, the present author forged ahead, determined and steadfast in his mission to chart a true *Map* that could lead us back through the *Gates* of the *Magic Kingdom* and retrieve the *Grail-secret* we had lost.

Finally, that *Map* has been rediscovered and decoded—and its facsimile stands publicly on display in these many printed works—for *anyone* that cares to travel this *Pathway*. The stable gains and progress you make on the *Pathway* is true and lasting—carried with you beyond this lifetime, on your infinite spiritual journey.

Now, the *Grail* is safely stored in the *Castle* again—an overflowing cup that serves to remind us that we already have, within our *Beingness*, the well-springs of *all the Havingness* we could ever want or dream for; and we have no need to be dependent on any other *Source.*

The *Grail* is there for all who might shed their *Human* garb, recollect the *fragmented pieces* of their *Beingness*, and simply *reach* through the dimensions for it. It is all of ours for the taking; and so long as this record is maintained, it can never be lost again.

But now I digress; yielding to the *next-generation* of *Seekers* to take up this quest and complete the *Pathway* for themselves —remembering always to *help one another.*

And to all those that follow: I have returned the *Sword* to the *Lake*—where it is now, still there, just waiting for *you.*

Safe journeys, dear Seeker.

We'll see you on the Other Side.

BASIC SYSTEMOLOGY GLOSSARY

actualization : to make actual, not just potential; to bring into full solid Reality; to realize fully in *Awareness* as a "thing."

agreement (reality) : unanimity of opinion of what is "thought" to be known; an accepted arrangement of how things are; things we consider as "real" or as an "is" of "reality"; a consensus of what is real as made by standard-issue (common) participants; what an individual contributes to or accepts as "real"; in *Systemology*, a synonym for "*reality.*"

alpha : the first, primary, basic, superior or beginning of some form; in *Systemology*, referring to the state of existence operating on spiritual archetypes and postulates, will and intention "exterior" to the low-level condensation and solidarity of energy and matter as the 'physical universe' (*beta*).

alpha-spirit : a "spiritual" *Life*-form; the "true" *Self* or I-AM; the *individual*; the spiritual (*alpha*) *Self* that is animating the (*beta*) physical body or "*genetic vehicle*" using a continuous *Lifeline* of spiritual ("*ZU*") energy; an individual spiritual (*alpha*) entity possessing no physical mass or measurable waveform (motion) in the Physical Universe as itself, so it animates the (*beta*) physical body or "*genetic vehicle*" as a catalyst to experience *Self*-determined causality in effect within the *Physical Universe*; a singular unit or point of *Spiritual Awareness* that is *Aware* that it is *Aware*.

alpha thought : the highest spiritual *Self-determination* over creation and existence exercised by an Alpha-Spirit; the Alpha range of pure *Creative Ability* based on direct postulates and considerations of *Beingness*; spiritual qualities comparable to "thought" but originating in Alpha-existence, independently superior to a Mind-System.

ascension : actualized *Awareness* elevated to the point of true "spiritual existence" exterior to *beta existence*. An "Ascended Master" is one who has returned to an incarnation on Earth as an inherently *Enlightened One*, demonstrable in their words and actions; they have the ability to *Self-direct* the "Mind" and "Body" as *Self* (as a "Spirit"); and to maintain consciousness as a personal identity continuum with the same *Self-directed* control and communication of Will-Intention that is exercised, actualized and developed deliberately during one's present incarnation.

associative knowledge : significance or meaning of a facet or aspect assigned to (or considered to have) a direct relationship with another facet; to connect or relate ideas or facets of existence with one another; in traditional systems logic, an equivalency of significance or meaning between facets or sets that are grouped together, such as in $(a + b) + c = a + (b + c)$; in Systemology, erroneous associative knowledge is assignment of the same value to all facets or parts considered as related (even when they are not actually so), such as in $a = a, b = a, c = a$ and so forth without distinction.

attention : active use of *Awareness* toward a specific aspect or thing; the act of "attending" with the presence of *Self*; a direction of focus or concentration of *Awareness* along a particular channel or conduit or toward a particular terminal node or communication termination point; the Self-directed concentration of personal energy as a combination of observation, thought-waves and consideration; focused application of *Self-Directed Awareness*.

awareness : the highest sense of-and-as *Self* in knowing and being as I-AM (the *Alpha-Spirit*); the extent of beingness directed as a viewpoint (POV) experienced by *Self* as *Knowingness*.

beta (awareness) : all consciousness activity ("*Awareness*") in the "Physical Universe" (KI,

286

in *Zuism*) or else in *beta-existence*; *Awareness* within the range of the *genetic-body*, including material thoughts, emotional responses and physical motors; personal *Awareness* of physical energy and physical matter moving through physical space and experienced as "time"; the *Awareness* held by *Self* that is restricted to an organic *Lifeform* or "*genetic vehicle*" in which it experiences causality in *beta-existence*.

beta (existence) : all manifestation in the "Physical Universe" (KI, in *Zuism*); the conditions of *Awareness* for the *Alpha-spirit* (*Self*) as a physical organic *Lifeform* or "*genetic vehicle*" in which it experiences causality in the *Physical Universe*.

charge : to fill or furnish with a quality; to supply with energy; to lay a command upon; in *Systemology*—to imbue with intention; to overspread with emotion; personal energy stores and significances entwined as fragmentation in mental images, reactive-response encoding and intellectual (and/or) programmed beliefs.

channel : a specific stream, course, current, direction or route; to form or cut a groove or ridge or otherwise guide along a specific course; a direct path; an artificial aqueduct created to connect two water bodies or water or make travel possible.

circuit : a circular path or loop; a closed-path within a system that allows a flow; a pattern or action or wave movement that follows a specific route or potential path only; in *Systemology*, "*communication processing*" pertaining to a specific *flow* of energy or information along a channel; "*feedback loop.*"

communication : successful transmission of information, data, energy (&tc.) along a message line, with a reception of feedback; an energetic flow of intention to cause an effect (or duplication) at a distance; the personal energy moved or acted upon by will or else 'selective directed attention'; the 'messenger action' used to transmit and receive energy across a medium; also relay of energy, a message or signal—or even locating a personal POV (viewpoint) for the Self—along the *ZU-line*.

condense (condensation) : the transition of vapor to liquid; denoting a change in state to a more substantial or solid condition; leading to a more compact or solid form.

confront : to come around in front of; to be in the presence of; to stand in front of, or in the face of; to meet "face-to-face" or "face-up-to"; additionally, in *Systemology*, to fully tolerate or acceptably withstand an encounter with a particular manifestation without an automatic reactive response.

consideration : careful analytical reflection of all aspects; deliberation; determining the significance of a "thing" in relation to similarity or dissimilarity to other "things"; evaluation of facts and importance of certain facts; thorough examination of all aspects related to, or important for, making a decision; the analysis of consequences and estimation of significance when making decisions; also in *Systemology*, the *postulate* or *Alpha-Thought* that defines the state of *beingness* for what something "*is.*"

defragmentation : the *reparation* of wholeness; collecting all dispersed parts to reform an original whole; a process of removing "*fragmentation*" in data or knowledge to provide a clear understanding; applying techniques and processes that promote a *holistic* interconnected *alpha* state, favoring observational *Awareness* of continuity in all spiritual and physical systems; in *Systemology*, a "*Seeker*" achieving actualized "*Self-Honest Awareness*" is said to be in a basic state of *beta-defragmentation*, whereas *Alpha-defragmentation* is the rehabilitation of the *creative ability*, managing the *Spiritual Timeline* and the POV of *Self* as Alpha-Spirit (I-AM).

existence : the *state* or fact of *apparent manifestation*; the resulting combination of the Principles of Manifestation: consciousness, motion and substance; continued *survival*; that which independently exists.

exterior : outside of; on the outside; in *Systemology*, we mean specifically the POV of *Self* that is *'outside of'* the *Human Condition,* free of the physical and mental trappings of the Physical Universe; a metahuman range of consideration; see also *'Zu-Vision'*.

external : a force coming from outside; information received from outside sources; in *Systemology*, the objective *'Physical Universe'* existence, or *beta-existence*, that the Physical Body or *genetic vehicle* is essentially *anchored* to for its considerations of locational space-time as a dimension or POV.

fragmentation : breaking into parts and scattering the pieces; the *fractioning* of wholeness or the *fracture* of a holistic interconnected *alpha* state, favoring observational *Awareness* of perceived connectivity between parts; *discontinuity*; separation of a totality into parts; in *Systemology*, a person outside of *Self-Honesty* is said to be operating from a *fragmented* state.

flow : movement across (or through) a channel (or conduit); a direction of active energetic motion, typically distinguished as either an *in-flow*, *out-flow* or *cross-flow*.

genetic-vehicle : a physical *Life*-form; the physical (*beta*) body that is animated/controlled by the (*Alpha*) *Spirit* using a continuous *Spiritual Lifeline* (ZU); a physical (*beta*) organic receptacle and catalyst for the (*Alpha*) *Self* to operate "causes" and experience "effects" within the *Physical Universe*.

harmful-act : a counter-survival mode of behavior or action (esp. that causes harm to one of more *Spheres of Existence*)—or—an overtly aggressive (hostile and/or destructive) action against an individual or any other *Sphere of Existence*; in *Utilitarian Systemology*—a short-sighted (serves fewest/lowest *Spheres of Existence*) intentional overtly harmful action to resolve a perceived problem; a revision of the rule for standard *Utilitarianism* for Systemology to distinguish actions which provide the least benefit to the least number of *Spheres of Existence*, or else the greatest harm to the greatest number of *Spheres of Existence*; in *moral philosophy*—an action which can be experienced by few and/or which one would not be willing to experience for themselves (*theft, slander, rape, &tc*); an iniquity or iniquitous act.

hold-back : withheld communications (esp. actions) such as "*Hold-Outs*"; intentional (or automatic) withdrawal (as opposed to reach); Self-restraint (which may eventually be enforced or automated); not reaching, acting or expressing, when one should be; an ability that is now restrained (on automatic) due to inability to withhold it on Self-determinism alone.

hold-outs : in photography, the numerous snapshots/pictures withheld from the final display or professional presentation of the event; withheld communications; in Utilitarian Systemology—energetic withdrawal and communication breaks with a "*terminal*" and its *Sphere of Existence* as a result of a "*Harmful-Act*"; unspoken or undiscovered (hidden, covert) actions that an individual withholds communications of, fearing punishment or endangerment of *Self-preservation* (*First Sphere*); the act of hiding (or keeping hidden) the truth of a "*Harmful-Act*"; a refusal to communicate with a *Pilot*; also "*Hold-Back.*"

holistic : the examination of interconnected systems as encompassing something greater than the *sum* of their "parts."

Human Condition : a standard default state of Human experience that is generally accepted to be the extent of its potential identity (*beingness*)—currently treated as *Homo Sapiens Sapiens,* but which is scheduled for replacement by *Homo Novus* (the "New Human").

imagination : ability to create *mental imagery* in one's Personal Universe at will and change or alter it as desired; the ability to create, change and dissolve mental images on command or as an act of will; to create a mental image or have associated imagery displayed (or "conjured") in the mind that may or may not be treated as real (or memory recall) and may or may not accurately duplicate objective reality; to employ *creative abilities* of the Spirit that are independent of reality agreements with beta-existence.

imprint : to strongly impress, stamp, mark (or outline) onto a softer 'impressible' substance; to mark with pressure onto a surface; in *Systemology*, used to indicate permanent Reality impressions marked by frequencies, energies or interactions experienced during periods of emotional distress, pain, unconsciousness, loss, enforcement, or something antagonistic to physical (personal) survival, all of which are are stored with other reactive response-mechanisms at lower-levels of *Awareness* as opposed to the active memory database and proactive processing center of the Mind; an experiential "memory-set" that may later resurface—be triggered or stimulated artificially—as Reality, of which similar responses will be engaged automatically; holographic-like imagery "stamped" onto consciousness as composed of energetic *facets* tied to the "snap-shot" of an experience.

imprinting incident : the first or original event

instance communicated and *emotionally encoded* onto an individual's "*Spiritual Timeline*" (recorded memory from all lifetimes), which formed a permanent impression that is later used to mechanistically treat future contact on that channel; the first or original occurrence of some particular *facet* or mental image related to a certain type of *encoded response*, such as pain and discomfort, losses and victimization, and even the acts that we have taken against others along the *Spiritual Timeline* of our existence that caused them to also be *Imprinted*.

intention : directed application of Will; to intend (have "in Mind") or signify (give "significance" to) for or toward a particular purpose; in *Systemology* (from the *Standard Model*)—the spiritual activity at WILL (5.0) directed by an *Alpha Spirit* (7.0); the application of WILL as "Cause" from a higher order of Alpha Thought and consideration (6.0).

interior : inside of; on the inside; in *Systemology*, we mean specifically the POV of *Self* that is fixed to the *'internal' Human Condition,* including the *Reactive Control Center* (RCC) and Mind-System or *Master Control Center* (MCC); within *beta-existence*.

internal : a force coming from inside; information received from inside sources; in *Systemology*, the objective experience of *beta-existence* associated with the Physical Body or *genetic vehicle* and its POV regarding sensation and perception; from inside the body; in the body.

invalidate : decrease the level or degree or *agreement* as Reality.

mental image : a subjectively experienced "picture" created and imagined into being by the Alpha-Spirit (or at lower levels, one of its automated mechanisms) that includes all perceptible *facets* of totally immersive scene, which may be forms originated by an individual, or a "facsimile-copy" ("snap-shot") of something seen or encountered; a duplication of wave-forms in one's Personal Universe as a "picture" that mirror an "external" Universe experience, such as an *Imprint*.

perception : internalized processing of data received by the *senses*; to become *Aware of* via the senses.

pilot : a professional steersman responsible for healthy functional operation of a ship toward a specific destination; in *Systemology*, an intensive trained individual qualified to specially apply *Systemology Processing* to assist other *Seekers* on the *Pathway*.

point-of-view (POV) : a point to view from; an opinion or attitude as expressed from a specific identity-phase; a specific standpoint or vantage-point; a definitive manner of consideration specific to an individual phase or identity; a place or position affording a specific view or vantage; circumstances and programming of an individual that is conducive to a particular response, consideration or belief-set (paradigm); a position (consideration) or place (location) that provides a specific view or perspective (subjective) on experience (of the objective).

postulate : to put forward as truth; to suggest or assume an existence *to be*; to state or affirm the existence of particular conditions; to provide a basis of reasoning and belief; a basic theory accepted as fact; in *Systemology*, Alpha-Thought —the top-most decisions or considerations made by the Alpha-Spirit regarding the "*isness*" (what things "are") about energy-matter and space-time.

presence : a quality of some thing (*energy/matter*) being "present" in space-time; personal orientation of *Self* as an *Awareness* (*POV*) located in present space-time (environment) and communicating with extant energy-matter.

processing command line (PCL) : a directed input; a specific command using highly selective language for *Systemology Processing*; a predetermined directive statement (cause) intended to focus concentrated attention (effect).

processing, systematic : the inner-workings or "through-put" result of systems; in *Systemology*, a method of applied spiritual technology used toward personal Self-Actualization; methods of selective directed attention, communicated language and associative imagery that increases personal control of the human condition.

realization : the clear perception of an understanding; a consideration or understanding on what is "actual"; to make "real" or give "reality" to so as to grant a property of "beingness" or "being as it is"; the state or instance of coming to an *Awareness*; in *Systemology*, "gnosis" or true knowledge achieved during *systematic processing*; achievement of a new (or higher) cognition, true knowledge or perception of Self; a consideration of reality or assignment of meaning.

responsibility : the *ability* to *respond*; the extent of mobilizing *power* and *understanding* an individual maintains as *Awareness* to enact *change*; the proactive ability to *Self-direct* and make decisions independent of an outside authority.

Seeker : an individual on the *Pathway to Self-Honesty*; a practitioner of *Mardukite Systemology* or *Systemology Processing*, that is working toward *Spiritual Ascension*.

Self-actualization : bringing the full potential of the Human spirit into Reality; expressing full capabilities and creativeness of the *Alpha-Spirit*.

Self-determinism : the freedom to act, clear of external control or influence; the personal control of Will to direct intention.

Self-honesty : the basic or original *alpha* state of *being* and *knowing*; clear and present total *Awareness* of-and-as *Self*, in its most basic and true proactive expression of itself as *Spirit* or *I-AM*—free of artificial attachments, perceptive filters and other emotionally-reactive or mentally-conditioned programming imposed on the human condition by the systematized physical world; the ability to experience existence without judgment.

spiritual timeline : a continuous stream of moment-to-moment *Mental Images* (or a record of experiences) that defines the "past" of a spiritual being (or *Alpha-Spirit*) and which includes impressions (*imprints, &tc.*) from all life-incarnations and significant spiritual events the being has encountered; in Systemology, also "*backtrack.*"

Spheres of Existence : a series of *eight* concentric circles, rings or spheres (each larger than the former) that is overlaid onto the Standard Model of Beta-Existence to demonstrate the dynamic systems of existence extending out from the POV of Self (often as a "body") at the *First Sphere*; these are given in the basic eightfold systems as: *Self, Home/Family, Groups, Humanity, Life on Earth, Physical Universe, Spiritual Universe* and *Infinity-Divinity.*

Systemology : a modern tradition of applied religious philosophy and spiritual technology based on *Arcane Tablets* (in combination with "*general systemology*" and "*games theory*") developed in the New Age underground by Joshua Free in 2011 as an advanced futurist extension of the *Mardukite Research Org.*

terminal (node) : a point, end, or mass, on a line; a connection point for closing an electric circuit, such as a post on a battery terminating at each end of its own systematic function; a point of connectivity with other points; in systems, a contact point of interaction; a point of interaction with other points.

turbulence : a quality or state of distortion or disturbance that creates irregularity of a flow or pattern; the quality or state of aberration on a line (such as ragged edges) or the emotional "turbulent feelings" attached to a particular flow or terminal node; a violent, haphazard or disharmonious commotion (such as in the ebb of gusts and lulls of wind action).

validation : a reinforcement of agreements or considerations as being "real."

viewpoint : see *"point-of-view" (POV)*.

willingness : the state of conscious Self-determined ability and interest (directed attention) to *Be*, *Do* or *Have*; a Self-determined consideration to reach, face up to (*confront*) or manage some "mass" or energy; the extent to which an individual considers themselves able to participate, act or communicate along some line, to put attention or intention on the line, or to produce (create) an effect.

ZU : the ancient Sumerian cuneiform sign for the archaic verb—*"to know," "knowingness"* or *"awareness"*; in *Mardukite Zuism and Systemology*, the active energy/matter of the "Spiritual Universe" (AN) experienced as a *Lifeforce* or *consciousness* that imbues living forms extant in the "Physical Universe" (KI); *"Spiritual Life Energy"*; energy demonstrated by the WILL of an actualized *Alpha-Spirit* in the "Spiritual Universe" (AN), which impinges its *Awareness* into the Physical Universe (KI), animating/controlling *Life* for its experience of *beta-existence* along an individual Alpha-Spirit's personal *Identity-continuum*, called a *ZU-line*.

Zu-Line : a theoretical construct in *Mardukite Zuism and Systemology* demonstrating *Spiritual*

Life Energy (*ZU*) as a personal individual "continuum" of Awareness interacting with all Spheres of Existence on the Standard Model of Systemology; a spectrum of potential variations and interactions of a monistic continuum or singular *Spiritual Life Energy* demonstrated on the Standard Model; an energetic channel of potential POV and "locations" of Beingness, demonstrated in early Systemology materials as an individual Alpha-Spirit's personal *Identity- continuum*, potentially connecting *Awareness* of *Self* with "*Infinity*" simultaneous with all points considered in existence; a symbolic demonstration of the "*Life-line*" on which *Awareness (ZU)* extends from the direction of the "Spiritual Universe" (AN) in its true original *alpha state* through an entire possible range of activity resulting in its *beta state* and control of a *genetic-entity* occupying the *Physical Universe (KI)*.

Zu-Vision : the true and basic (*Alpha*) Point-of-View (perspective, POV) maintained by *Self* as *Alpha-Spirit* outside boundaries or considerations of the *Human Condition* and *exterior* to beta-existence reality agreements with the Physical Universe; a POV of Self *as* "a unit of Spiritual Awareness" that exists independent of a "body" and entrapment in a *Human Condition*; "spirit vision" in its truest sense.

Collector's Edition Hardcover

THE FUNDAMENTALS OF
SYSTEMOLOGY

A Basic Course developed by
Joshua Free

*collecting material of six lesson-booklets
together in one volume!*

"Being More Than Human"

"Realities in Agreement"

"Windows To Experience"

"Ancient Systemology"

"A History of Systemology"

"Systemology Processing"

All *six* lesson-booklets of the first official
Basic Course on Mardukite Systemology
are combined together in *one volume* as
"Fundamentals of Systemology."

Lesson booklets are also available individually!

Collector's Edition Hardcover

THE PATHWAY TO
ASCENSION

The Official 2024 Systemology
Professional Course by
Joshua Free

All sixteen lessons available in two volumes!

"Increasing Awareness"

"Thought & Emotion"

"Clear Communication"

"Handling Humanity"

"Free Your Spirit"

"Escaping Spirit-Traps"

"Eliminating Barriers"

"Conquest of Illusion"

All *sixteen* lesson-booklets of the newest
Professional Course on Mardukite Systemology
are combined together in *two volumes* as
"The Pathway to Ascension."

Lesson booklets are also available individually!

Collector's Edition Hardcover

KEYS TO THE

KINGDOM

The Official Systemology
Advanced Training Course by
Joshua Free

All eight A.T. manuals available in two volumes!

"The Secret of Universes"

"Games, Goals and Purposes"

"The Jewel of Knowledge"

"Implanted Universes"

"Entities and Fragments"

"Spiritual Perception"

"Mastering Ascension"

"Advancing Systemology"

All *eight* A.T. manuals of the *New Standard*
Systemology *Advanced Training Course*
along with *three* training supplements
are combined together
in *two volumes* as
"Keys to the Kingdom."

Manuals are also available as individual booklets!

THE SYSTEM

Seekers and students of the *Professional Course* and *Advanced Training Course* will also be interested in the original *Systemology Core Research Series*. These 8 volumes are a complete chronological record of *Mardukite NexGen New Thought* developments published by the *Systemology Society* from 2019 through 2023.

The *Systemology Core* series begins with the first professional publication released when our *Mardukite Systemology* emerged from the underground in 2019, with: *"The Tablets of Destiny Revelation."*

OLOGY CORE

The Tablets of Destiny Revelation:
*How Long-Lost Anunnaki Wisdom
Can Change the Fate of Humanity*

Crystal Clear: *Handbook for Seekers*

Metahuman Destinations (2 *volumes*)

Imaginomicon:
Approaching Gateways to Higher Universes

Way of the Wizard: *Utilitarian Systemology*

Systemology-180: *Fast-Track to Ascension*

Systemology Backtrack:
Reclaiming Spiritual Power & Past-Life Memory

PUBLISHED BY THE **JOSHUA FREE** IMPRINT REPRESENTING

The Mardukite Academy of Systemology

mardukite.com

www.ingramcontent.com/pod-product-compliance
Lightning Source LLC
Chambersburg PA
CBHW061138120626
46546CB00005B/1833